Children Helping Children with Grief

My Path to Founding The Dougy Center for Grieving Children and Their Families

BEVERLY J. CHAPPELL

Foreword by Earl A. Grollman

NewSage Press
Troutdale, Oregon

Children Helping Children with Grief

Paperback Original ISBN 978-0-939165-54-4

NewSage Press
PO Box 607
Troutdale, OR 97060-0607
503-695-2211
www.newsagepress.com

Book design and cover by Sherry Wachter

Printed in the United States
Distributed in the United States and Canada by
Publishers Group West 800-788-3123

Library of Congress Cataloging-in-Publication Data

Chappell, Beverly J., 1930-
Children helping children with grief : my path to founding the Dougy Center for Grieving Children and Their Families / Beverly J. Chappell ; foreword by Earl A. Grollman.
p. cm.
Includes index.
ISBN 978-0-939165-54-4
1. Dougy Center for Grieving Children and Their Families. 2. Children and death. 3. Grief in children. 4. Bereavement in children. 5. Children's drawings. 6. Kübler-Ross, Elisabeth. I. Title.
BF723.D3C43 2007
155.9'37083--dc22

2007036097

1 2 3 4 5 6 7 8 9 10

A simple child,
that simply draws its breath,
And feels its life in every limb,
What should it know of death?

—William Wordsworth

Acknowledgments

This book has been quite a project for me, and for my publisher. A special thanks to Maureen Michelson, my editor and publisher at NewSage Press, for your supreme efforts on the book—and for hanging in there with me. You have been an incredibly patient teacher. I feel more blessed than you can ever know! I also want to acknowledge NewSage Press designer, Sherry Wachter, for her creative talents in designing this beautiful book.

My heartfelt gratitude goes to all of the children and their families who allowed me to use their stories, for your stories are the book. Your honesty—and the pain surrounding your stories—has helped this book become an accurate picture of what children's grief is really about. This book has also allowed me, through you, to share those immediate emotions of your loss. Most of all I am grateful to the children who have been willing to teach me all about their grief, and how to be more effective in helping them ease that pain of loss and begin to heal.

Many thanks to all of you—board members, volunteers, facilitators, staff members—who generously contributed your stories for the book. Your memories and perspectives helped bring this book to life. And without you there would be no support program. In particular, I want to acknowledge Bev Fulk who co-founded The Dougy Center with me. Without her I would never have had the courage to begin this formidable project by myself. Thanks, Bev, wherever you may be.

The ten-year-old students at the Whitman School workshop opened my eyes to the depth of unmet, unspoken, and unshared childhood grief. Without their honesty in sharing their pain, sadness, and anger about the deaths that affected them so deeply, I would never have known. To this day, their spontaneous drawings move me when I look at them, almost thirty years later. I will always be grateful to these wise and courageous children.

The Dougy Center would never have succeeded without the prodding, belief, encouragement, and love of our precious friend, Elisabeth Kübler-Ross. Nor would it have come into being without the help and encouragement of my loving and supporting husband, Allan

Chappell, who walked every step of the way with me until his death. My gratitude for these two special people lives in my heart, always.

A special "thank you" to the Omega Foundation in London, England, for their generous grant that helped bring this book to fruition; especially to Christopher Donovan, Ph.D. and Gregg Furth, Ph.D. The Omega Foundation was established by Susan Bach, Ph.D., who was Gregg's teacher and mentor in the art of interpretation of spontaneous drawings. And Gregg was my teacher.

Last, but by no means least, thank you to Brian Allen who took my place this year as Chair of the Trustees at church so I could finish my book.

BEVERLY J. CHAPPELL
December, 2007

Contents

PART ONE
My Path to The Dougy Center

COLOR IMAGES

Part Two
The Dougy Center

Foreword

When the history of the Death and Dying Movement is listed, Beverly Chappell's name will be among the most prominent. Many of us have written books on children and grief. Bev has created those tools to help grieving youngsters with a revolutionary self-help support group called The Dougy Center. These engaging pages tell her remarkable story of founding The Dougy Center.

Children Helping Children with Grief is a candid and courageous account of one woman's struggle to cope with the taboo subject—children and grief. Bev teaches us that just as we cannot protect ourselves from life, so we cannot protect young people from the reality of death. Traumatic experiences belong to both adulthood and childhood. The worst enemy is our secrecy when we try to pretend that children's lives are unchanged and there are no avenues for them to cope with their tragedy. The Dougy Center has shown us there is a way to support children in their grief and loss. Today, this premiere support group offers a model that is being used internationally.

This book is so highly readable yet so very profound. Bev's style is neither complex or esoteric. She writes powerfully with penetrating perspectives coupled with practical advice. Bev brings a depth of meaning and purpose with incisive drawings and images, along with true-life stories of the children and adolescents. You will be mesmerized by her genuineness and steadfastness. Reading this book is like spending a long, invaluable time with a trusted companion who has invited you to enter her significant life's work.

The chapters are filled with both pain and triumph, and most of all characterized by the rarest of qualities—wisdom and love. The book is a gem to be treasured.

RABBI EARL A. GROLLMAN, DHL; DD
Author, *Talking about Death—A Dialogue*
Between Parents and Children and
Straight Talk About Death for Teenagers

See This Child

See this child before you
   wounded
   vulnerable
   changed
...the child of yesterday gone forever
Who will really look at this child?
   Is it easier to assume that
   he will emerge unscathed,
   than to face the turmoil within him?
Who will step into the road
   before this child...
   laden with mountains and valleys,
   potholes and detours?
Who will walk a bit of his journey with him?
Who will offer some temporary shelter
   from the storms that rage around
   and within this child?
Who will open doors that this child
   cannot see through his pain?
Who will listen to what this child
   is really saying
   when he is belligerent
   when he is too shy to speak
   when his laughter masks his fears?
Who will help this child to recognize
   his successes,
   and give him courage to step
   beyond his failures with dignity?
Who will be with this child
   on the other side of healing
   as he recognizes his growth
   and acceptance?

UNKNOWN
(A handout at the World Gathering on Bereavement)

PART ONE

My Path to The Dougy Center

Bev Chappell

Since my first days as an
eighteen-year-old nursing student
I felt drawn to the dying patients
and I was always comfortable
being with them.

Bev Chappell

CHAPTER ONE

Inspiration

For far too long people did not die. Instead, they were "lost to us," "went on a long trip," "went to sleep," "passed on," "passed over" or "passed away." Unfortunately, that is often still the case today. These euphemisms were, and continue to be, the walls that cut us off from death and dying, and the subsequent grief for those facing the death of a loved one.

In the early 1950s when I was a student nurse, there was no Dr. Elisabeth Kübler-Ross to advocate for dying patients or their families. It was unheard of for nurses and doctors to provide a family with support through the grief that followed a death. In fact, when I was a student nurse it was an offense to give extra, or even adequate care to a dying patient when there was a post-surgical or new admission patient on the care list. More than once I was reprimanded for spending too much time with a dying patient. It was not unusual for a dying patient to be placed in the room farthest from the nurses' desk and frequently the last call light on the floor to be answered.

After a patient died, it was the norm to close all the doors to the other patients' rooms on the hospital floor before attendants wheeled the sheet-covered body on a gurney down the hallway to the morgue in the basement. The hospital administration determined that the sight of a dead body would be too upsetting.

During my years as a nursing student and later as a young registered nurse, two of the worst polio epidemics in the United States took place. My husband-to-be, Allan Chappell, who was a physician in pediatric residency at the time, worked eighteen-to-twenty hour days caring for polio patients. It was common for us as hospital staff to work long hours. Many patients died; most of them were children and teens.

There was never any emotional aftercare for these families. They were all on their own: Parents whose children had died; children whose fathers or mothers had died; siblings whose brothers or sisters had died. No one took these grieving parents or children under their wings. And certainly, no one ever acknowledged that doctors and nurses might be grieving as they faced the deaths of so many patients during these epidemics. The hospital chaplains, counselors, and personnel from the funeral homes all went about their business, ignoring the grief that shadowed their daily work. We all seemed to be the walking wounded, isolated and grief-stricken.

Since my first days as an eighteen-year-old nursing student I felt drawn to the dying patients and I was always comfortable being with them. From the beginning, it was not unusual for me to spend extra time with these particular patients. One day, early in my floor duty experience, I arrived at work to learn one of my favorite patients was close to death. She had a heart condition, hypertension, and kidney failure. Before long she was in a coma. In recent weeks, we had become especially close for a student and a patient, perhaps in part because she had no family and no visitors. In addition, she had been an industrial nurse at Meredith Publishing Company in Des Moines, Iowa, and we had several chats about what her nurse's training was like when she was young.

The day she was dying I stayed at her bedside longer than usual. At one point the doctor came into the room when she was very near death. He told me, "Go to lunch and on to class. There is nothing more you can do for her." He left, but I didn't. I stayed, wiping the uremic frost from her face with a warm wet washcloth. Until she died, I sat by the bed and held her hand.

As was required, I reported the death to the head nurse. When she saw me, she asked with a critical tone, "Miss Rosene, why are you still on the floor? Why aren't you in class where you belong?" That was the first of several similar situations in which I could have been expelled from training and sent home.

On another occasion I was lucky and did not get caught assisting a dying patient. I was working the night shift, alone, on the hospital's small west wing predominantly occupied by elderly and dying patients—except for one. A young man in his late twenties was dying of leukemia. In the 1950s, hospital rules forbade small children to visit patients and strictly limited the number of adult visitors to specific visiting hours. One night the young man's wife slipped into his room after the strictly controlled visiting hours were over. I decided not to ask her to leave. She sat with her husband, held his hand, and they talked about their children. For a time she laid on the bed beside him. Before the hospital supervisor appeared on her morning rounds I hurried the wife out the emergency exit. Before she left I promised I would let her back in through the hospital's emergency door that night at a specific time. I encouraged her to bring their two children so they could spend time with their father.

That night his wife returned with their two small children who were four and six years old. They were delighted to see their daddy. They crawled on the bed, curled up in his arms, and fell asleep. It did not frighten them that he was dying. I realized somehow they were very wise for their young ages. Their mom must have talked to them about Daddy's dying, and they seemed to know how to be present for every sacred moment with him. Many nights when I was on duty, I let them in to be with their dad. In less than two weeks he died.

At the time I wondered why I had provided the opportunity for this family to be together while the father was dying. It would have meant certain death to my nursing career if I had been caught. I always knew I had been a rebel where death was concerned. Intuitively, I must have known then what I now know without a doubt—children and families need the support and the time to experience their grief in their own time, both during a loved one's dying and after.

Confusing Children About Death

Over the years I met many children who had experienced the death of a parent or sibling and they had never grieved. I also met many adults who, when they were young, had experienced the death of a parent or sibling and had never grieved openly with their surviving family, or with anyone else. Tragically, some grief-stricken and confused children were never told what had happened to the family member who had disappeared from their lives. Parents often put away photos of the deceased and/or never spoke the dead person's name again, making the situation even eerier for those children. The bewildered expressions and feelings of loss I witnessed on so many children's faces haunted me.

Sometimes when a parent was dying of an incurable illness, well-meaning adults sent the children away from home to stay with family or friends. The children would not return home until after the death of the parent, and oftentimes not until after the memorial service. When children asked where a parent had gone, too many were given strange, unbelievable, and even untrue responses. "Dad went away on a long trip" or "Mom went to visit a cousin." Sometimes the adults would never even discuss why a parent was no longer present in the home. Many times the common answer to a child's question of where a parent or a sibling had gone was to tell them, "They have gone to heaven." For children whose family followed no particular religion, they often had no idea where heaven was. It could have been New Jersey as far as the children were concerned, and they didn't know where that was either.

One time while I was sitting in a room filled with family members grieving the death of a grandfather, a grandchild walked in and asked why everyone was so sad. The reply was, "We have lost Grandpa." Worried, the child quickly responded, "We need to go find him."

In the Beginning

Grieving children and families continued to cross my path through my husband's work as a pediatrician. Even with families in my own neighborhood, tragedy would strike, and all too often the children's grief and needs were completely unrecognized. Wherever I looked, there seemed to be an endless stream of grieving kids and their families whose needs were not being met. They were really on their own.

After our first child, Kathy, was born in 1953 my husband strongly encouraged me to quit my work as a nurse and stay home. I agreed to stay home and be a full-time Mom. This decision had been influenced by unfinished grief—my husband's. Allan was only thirteen years old when his mother died after a long struggle with breast cancer. Those teen years were agonizing for Allan and his sister, who was two years younger. Both children felt lost without their caring and loving mother. Their dad, as is often the case, remarried soon after his wife's death. This new stepmother truly rivaled Cinderella's. So, much later as I began to identify others' unspoken and unresolved grief and loss, I could also see how it had played out in my own family.

On Allan's $125.00 a month pediatric residency salary and our $75 a month rent, my not going back to work was a financial catastrophe, but somehow we made it. Ultimately, I was grateful to stay home with my children, even though I was not practicing nursing. My profession became that of a pediatrician's wife and phone answerer. There were no pagers, no cell phones, and no answering service for private practice physicians in the 1950s. In those days, Allan encouraged patients to call our house after hours if they needed help, and I often felt like his at-home nurse. When Allan wasn't home or at the hospital after hours, he was often making house calls. In 1956, our second child, Steven, was born and my full time job as a mother and a physician's wife kept my days full for years.

One of My Most Significant Grief Teachers

In the early 1970s, I realized it would not be long until the primary focus of my life, two active and very busy teenagers, would be flying from the nest. I wondered what I would do when I no longer had to take care of my children on a daily basis and be involved with their many activities. I had not done any nursing in years so it would be necessary to take a refresher course even though my Iowa license was current. However, after taking the required refresher course, I was clear that I did not want to return to traditional nursing.

In September 1971, our son's best friend, Brian, faced a traumatic family situation. Brian was like a part of our family, often joining us on our family vacations. Brian's mother had been struggling with pain and nausea for at least six months. No one took her seriously and she received the medical run around—"it's all in your head" type of thing. Finally, she had major surgery and the doctors found uterine cancer that had already spread to her intestine. For the next thirteen months, she was in treatment with frequent stays in the hospital. At sixteen years old, Brian was just learning to drive so my husband, our daughter Kathy, or I became his transportation so he could visit his mother.

Brian's parents were divorced, and Brian's dad offered no emotional support whatsoever. A sister, twelve years older, and a brother, six years older, lived out of the area. The brother seldom came to visit during the thirteen-month cancer fight and Brian's sister came occasionally, but reluctantly. During his mother's illness and hospitalizations, Brian spent long hours at lunchtime and well into the night at her bedside. He hated watching his mom suffer through her illness. He would stay with her holding the emesis basin when she vomited, and then get her settled. Once she was comfortable, Brian would run to the bathroom and vomit.

Even in exhaustion and in the beginnings of illness himself, Brian would not let me call his school to allow him a morning off or to come in late without penalty. He did not want the school to know what was happening in his life. Brian did not want to be different from his peers. Little did I know then that Brian's response is absolutely normal for most teens and children, even as young as six. Whether it is a loved one who is dying or someone who has died, children do not generally make this a subject for conversation. I now understand that this is a means of protection for them as well as for those around them. Young people also know that their peers can say and do cruel things to those who have suffered the death of a loved one. What children may not know is that cruelty can be rooted in the other person's own grief and ignorance, or fear.

In the end, Brian, his sister, and I were at their mom's bedside when she died. Following her death, Brian lived alone in the home he and his mother had shared. His father lived in another part of the city and supported Brian financially so he could remain in the same school district, but offered little more. Our family became Brian's main source of support and comfort. As soon as Brian's mother died we invited him to live with us. Four months later Brian decided to live with us until he graduated from high school.

During Brian's mother's final illness and death, I was fully reintroduced to the world of doctors, nurses, hospitals, pain, and dying. This rekindled a passion of mine first sparked in my early nursing career—concern for the dying patient. I did not realize at the time that Brian was to become one of the most incredible teachers in my life. Brian would teach me about children and teens in the process of anticipatory grief and the grief following death. It would be years later before I would more fully understand the pain, agony, and aloneness Brian had endured.

During this time with Brian, I would come to know for certain what I wanted and needed to do with my life. Before long I would meet a wonderful friend and mentor, Elisabeth Kübler-Ross, M.D. She, too, would offer much needed inspiration and guidance. My time with Brian was a perfect example of what Elisabeth Kübler-Ross repeated so often: *When the student is ready, the teacher will appear.*

I have never met a person whose greatest need was
anything other than real, unconditional love.
You can find it in a simple act of kindness
toward someone who needs help.
There is no mistaking love.

You feel it in your heart. It is the common fiber of life,
the flame that heals our soul, energizes our spirit
and supplies passion to our lives. It is our
connection to God and to each other.

ELISABETH KÜBLER-ROSS

CHAPTER TWO

Elisabeth Kübler-Ross:
Mentor and Friend

During the hospital experiences for Brian's mom, I had considerable time to observe that little had changed since my student nursing days regarding the doctors' and nurses' acceptance and care of a dying patient. After deciding I did not want to continue my nursing career, I began speaking to psychology and health classes at Portland State University (PSU) about death and dying, urging them to think about the things they might need to do if they found out they had only a short time to live. I had started in this direction at the suggestion of Peter Peth, Ph.D. who wanted to impact his students with the fact that life does not go on forever.

A number of Dr. Peth's students from that class wanted to form a group to do more in-depth thinking about not only death and dying, but life and living: learning how to make the most of the time they had right now. We met for three terms at Koinonia House on the PSU campus. When the school year ended, we did not want to disband. We had become an intimate group, openly sharing and discussing thoughts and fears about death, and learning to make the most of life. Most of the group began to meet twice a month in Allan's and my home. One of the students that affected the group the most and was most influenced by our gatherings was Becky, a young woman in her early twenties. Becky and I became good friends.

Becky, at age twelve, had developed aplastic anemia after having been given treatment with Chloromycetin for meningitis. After the group was no longer meeting in our home, I still continued to be a part of Becky's life, through much of her illness, and eventual death. In the process of working with Becky, my interest in the dying patient was further renewed and I befriended several people in their dying process. The idea of working with a dying patient was a totally new concept for hospital staff and most times, unacceptable. They did not think such patient care was necessary. By some unexplainable efforts, I did work my way into Portland Adventist Hospital through the Director of Social Work, Ed Cochrane, and together we saw many terminally ill and dying patients. After a time, the nursing staff started calling me to visit patients who were in the last stages of their diseases, and life. Eventually, a few of the nurses were delighted to have me available to help dying patients.

In October 1973, there was a course offered by the Oregon Council of Churches, now called Ecumenical Ministries. It was a twelve-week course, "Issues of Death and Dying." I persuaded my husband to attend this class with me, thinking it would be valuable for both of us. Allan had been uncomfortable with death ever since the death of his mother. In addition, Allan had two young girls as pediatric patients who had died of different types of cancer. Allan was eager to find help for the grieving families and for himself.

In my own life, I had struggled with my griefs as well. My only sibling, a younger brother, David, had died tragically in 1968 after struggling for years with drug abuse. I found myself just wanting to wash my hands of his troubled life, while at the same time carrying a deep sadness for memories of the brilliant sweet brother who was charming and loved by everyone who had known him. He had a beautiful voice and had sung in both the Navy Choir and church choirs. David was twenty-eight when he died. I was left with a strange numbness and disconnect after years of witnessing his troubled life, telling myself I had no great grief over my brother's death. His death was devastating to my parents who had each had severe losses as children, and they had wanted a son more than anything.

In this "Issues of Death and Dying" course taught by Chaplain Horace Duke, we used Elisabeth Kübler-Ross' book, *On Death and Dying*, as the text. My spark of interest soon became a roaring fire of desire to learn all I could about death, dying, and grief. Dr. Ross' writings were an affirmation that the things I had done on the sly for patients and their families as a student nurse years earlier were okay, and ahead of their time.

After reading *On Death and Dying*, I felt I had met a kindred spirit in Elisabeth Kübler-Ross. I begged my husband to write to Dr. Ross on my behalf, thinking that if she received a letter from another physician rather than a note from me, a nurse, she would be more likely to respond. My husband sent her a letter in February 1974: "My wife is an R.N. who has taken time out to raise our children," Allan wrote. "She is now very interested in working with dying patients and their families. Could you give us some information on where in our area she might get that learning and experience?"

In less than a month, a handwritten letter arrived with Dr. Ross' response. "I vill be in Valla Valla, Vashington the first veekend in April. If you can come to my vorkshop, I vill be glad to talk vith you." Allan and I smiled at the fact that she even wrote with a Swiss accent, using a "v" instead of a "w."

Becoming Friends

When we met Elisabeth Kübler-Ross on April 5, 1974 in Walla Walla, Washington, I felt jolted into a new life direction. From the moment I saw Elisabeth walk to the platform to speak, I knew she would be my mentor and guide for the journey ahead of me. What I did not expect was Elisabeth becoming a beloved family friend. More than thirty years later I still consider Elisabeth my guide and dear friend, even in the years since her death. When I first met Elisabeth, I had no idea what our journey would encompass, but I knew immediately it would be phenomenal and I would learn more than I could imagine.

After first meeting Elisabeth, she sent us information on her one-week workshop in Santa Barbara, California and urged us to attend. My husband and I did

Bev and Allan Chappell with Elisabeth Kübler-Ross, June 1974.

11

attend that workshop in June 1974, never dreaming where it would lead. At the workshop's end, I had an opportunity to tell Elisabeth that our daughter, Kathy, had been diagnosed with an extremely rare, incurable, life-threatening disease just five days after we had first met Elisabeth in Walla Walla. I also talked with her about my husband being in denial about Kathy's disease. He refused to talk about it with Kathy, or with me.

Allan was able to face death, even though it had been difficult, but the potential death of his daughter from a disease of which we had never heard was too much to face. Elisabeth asked around for a piece of paper and a pencil—she never carried any excess baggage—and wrote down her address in Flossmoor, Illinois, and her private phone number. "You can always reach me if you need me," she said as she handed me the paper. "If I am not there, my family vill know how to reach me. Be sure to call. Do you hear me?" That day became the first of many times Elisabeth would reach out to me unconditionally. She would always be no further than a phone call away.

The following week Allan and I talked at length with our daughter's dermatologist who had given us the diagnosis. Since so little was known about Kathy's rare disease, the doctor encouraged us to stay calm until we could find more up-to-date information. That was hard to do, but we did our best. Six weeks after her diagnosis, Kathy decided to leave home for Seattle to teach figure skating. She was twenty years old, full of life and her future. I knew Kathy deserved to live her life with the quality she desired. Over time, my husband did come to terms with the disease and the way Kathy wanted to handle it. When Kathy got a new physician in Seattle she learned about research being done in Denver, Colorado. She became involved in that research with her doctor's help. (As of 2007, Kathy is doing great, and concern has almost disappeared about what might happen to her because of this disease.)

Before I even considered taking up Elisabeth's offer to call if I needed her, she called me. She was working on her new book, *Death: The Final Stage of Growth*, and she asked if I, as a nurse, would read two of her chapters and give her my opinion. I was honored that she would ask for my assistance. From this proof reading, our friendship grew. I had placed Elisabeth on a high pedestal; almost untouchable, and yet, she was reaching out to me as a friend. In time, our friendship grew close and it became special for both of us in many ways. Elisabeth loved my husband dearly, and our children, as well.

I attended three more of Elisabeth's one-week workshops, learning more about death and dying. One of them was held at Menucha, a conference center perched high on the southwest edge of the Columbia River Gorge, about twenty-five minutes from downtown Portland. The Gorge with its many waterfalls reminded Elisabeth of her home in Switzerland and she loved this conference setting. On one occasion when I did not attend one of her Menucha workshops, she called me and said she needed to get away for the afternoon. Elisabeth had given the attendees a big project to work on and told them to have it ready for presentation that evening. She explained to me on the phone, "That will keep them busy while I'm not here."

I drove out and got her. Elisabeth wanted to go to a shopping center, so we drove to one in Northeast Portland. She was like a little kid on an exciting adventure. First, Elisabeth went to a candy store and bought several pounds of chocolates, even though she constantly commented that no chocolate was as good as the chocolate she could get in Switzerland. Then she spotted a hardware store. Her eyes lit up and a grin spread across her face. "Ve must go to the hardvare store," she said gleefully. Elisabeth moved through the hardware store like a child turned loose at a carnival. In all my years of knowing her, I do not believe I ever saw her have so much fun. I followed her around as she put things she intended to buy in my arms. She bought fireplace tools (for a fireplace she did not have) and gardening tools. Elisabeth loved gardening and canning the things she grew. I didn't have a clue, nor did Elisabeth, how she was going to get all her purchases on the plane back to San Diego. At one point I asked, "Elisabeth, how are you going to get all of this home?" She smiled a joyous smile and insisted, "Ve vill find a vay."

On the way back to Menucha Conference Center Elisabeth wanted to stop at the Vista House parking lot to see the wonderful view of the mighty Columbia River. The wind was blowing down the Gorge and we could hardly stand up without being blown backward. It was like standing in a wind tunnel. I was trying unsuccessfully to get a scarf tied over my teased, back combed, and sprayed hair. Elisabeth looked at me quizzically as I struggled with the scarf, her own hair flying freely about her face. Then, she reached over and ran her fingers through my hair, declaring, "Don't vorry about your hair. Look at this magnificent scene." That was the last time I ever had my hair back combed, teased, and hair sprayed. Once again, Elisabeth reminded me of what was important, and especially what was not.

It took one specific occasion to prove to me how in tune Elisabeth and I were with each other. This particular incident boggled my mind, and still does. It was just before Memorial Day 1980, and I was standing at the kitchen counter cutting up cooked potatoes for a potato salad. The task seemed to take forever because my heart was not into cooking. The phone rang, and with wet and slippery hands I answered. A familiar voice asked, "Vhat has happened? You are so on my mind and I couldn't vait to get to my center to call you. I just got off the plane from Australia and knew I had to call right avay."

Elisabeth's perceptiveness took my breath away. Yes, something had happened, but how did she know? I had just returned from Iowa. My father had died of a cardiac arrest and I had gone back for a couple of weeks to attend the funeral and to help my mother after the rest of the family had returned home. It had been difficult, as usual, helping my mom, who always insisted on perfection. No one could ever do things right—meaning her way—and I had spent a lifetime trying to be perfect to please my mom. Old and deep-seated grief rose up for me as I grappled with my father's death. For a lifetime, I felt that I was not the son my parents had hoped and longed for—and their only son had died twelve years earlier! My parents cared for and loved me, but their disappointment was always there, throughout my life, just below the surface.

Admittedly, I was both delighted and guilty to be back home with Allan and our son. Kathy was married and living in Seattle. When I told Elisabeth about my father's death, she said she had known it was something serious. She gave me the consolation that I so desperately needed, knowing what was helpful to say at such a time.

Over the years, Elisabeth embraced my family and me, finding ways to express her friendship and love, despite a fast lifestyle and tremendous international presence. One time when she was in Portland for a lecture, Allan and I drove Elisabeth to the airport and we waited with her at the gate. In the course of conversation, Allan told Elisabeth about our new granddaughter, Courtney. Elisabeth asked him if he had a photo, explaining that "all good grandpas should have photos." Allan did have a special photo of baby Courtney lying on her tummy on Allan's knees. Elisabeth asked him if she could have it. How could Allan refuse?

Elisabeth Kübler-Ross and Bev Chappell at The Dougy Center, 1985.

Perhaps there was a special kinship because both Allan and Elisabeth, as physicians, had an affinity for caring at a deep level about their patients and their families. She sent him notes and on two different occasions, sun-prints of dainty flowers or weeds she had learned how to make. Often, when Elisabeth called our home she asked to chat with Allan after we had finished talking. Allan was special to Elisabeth.

A Place for Grieving Children

When Elisabeth was in Portland in 1981, we talked about my work with families who had a parent or a child dying. I observed that after the death the children in those families seemed to need special help with their grief that they were not receiving. In particular, I had observed that in most cases children were unable to talk to a parent about their loss. If the other parent or a sibling had died, the children worried about making the parent(s) cry so they held in all their questions and grief. And if they did ask questions, they did not ask for long if no one answered. Elisabeth had her own thinking about people asking questions that she called "My Rule of Three." She believed if you ask a question three times and it isn't answered, it will not be. The children seem to know subconsciously that three times was all they would ask, and they would not ask again.

I could see it was terribly scary for children to think they caused a parent to cry. When I explained this, Elisabeth immediately asked, "Vhat vill make it better?" I replied, "I think they need a place where they can talk about what happened with other kids of comparable ages who have had a comparable death in their lives. Children need to share their pain, emptiness, and anger without thinking they are causing everyone even more pain by making their parents cry." Without a moment's hesitation, Elisabeth looked at me and said, "You make that place." I was stunned! She continued, "You get started. I vil help you." And she did.

On December 29, 1982, a few of us who learned the skills of facilitating at workshops began the first group for grieving children, which was the beginning of The Dougy Center. Four boys who had experienced the death of their fathers arrived at my home accompanied by their mothers. (See Chapter Twelve, "First Support Groups.")

Over the years, Elisabeth kept in constant touch with me to see how things were going at The Dougy Center, as well as with me as her friend. She pointed us in several directions where she believed we could write grants for funding and often sent words of encouragement and ideas for the program at the center. Elisabeth gave a lecture in Portland as a fund raiser for The Dougy Center, raising much-needed funds as well as attracting national media attention for the Center.

From the beginning of The Dougy Center, we listed her name on the Honorary and Advisory Boards. Elisabeth was the one who connected me with Doug Turno, the courageous boy who deeply inspired my work with grieving children. She also sent Izetta Smith to me when Izetta was taking one of Elisabeth's workshops on the East coast, and that was a miracle in itself. Izetta became a member of the first parents' group, as well as one of the first facilitators. Her son came to The Dougy Center for a children's group after the death of his dad.

Elisabeth's Final Years

In 1983, Elisabeth bought a three-hundred-acre farm in Head Waters, Virginia. Eventually, she built a wonderful huge log cabin, raised llamas—her favorite soft and gentle animals—and had a Saint Bernard. In 1990, she moved her healing center, Shanti Nilaya (Home of Peace) from Escondido, California to her farm, which became her new center,

Elisabeth in front of her log cabin in Virginia with her St. Bernard, Victor, 1987.

The Elisabeth Kübler-Ross Center. She continued offering her one-week workshops, training professionals and laypersons alike to work with the terminally ill.

Often, Elisabeth has been credited with bringing the concept of hospice to the United States from its origins in England. Elisabeth hoped to build a hospice for orphaned babies who had AIDS. When news of Elisabeth's plans spread, neighbors and community members were strongly opposed. In 1994, while she was in Europe giving several workshops and visiting her family in Switzerland, tragedy hit her center. When Elisabeth returned, she found her home and healing center in smoldering ashes, burned to the ground, and one of her llamas had been shot. Elisabeth's manuscripts, international research on death, and personal belongings burned in the fire. All that was left were the clothes on her back and in her small suitcase.

After that, Elisabeth decided to hand over the operation of the center to an executive director. A short time later, she had a massive brainstem stroke, and then another, which most people do not survive. After a short period of medical treatment, Elisabeth moved to Arizona to be near her son, Ken Ross, where she found herself a "perfect house out in the desert" that she purchased. She spent a lot of time healing and enjoying the simple pleasures of her home, such as feeding the coyotes at her back door and watching rattlesnakes unsuccessfully try to get food out of the bird feeders.

People in great numbers visited Elisabeth. One in particular, Joanne Cacciatore, founder of The MISS Foundation (formerly Mothers in Sympathy and Support) for parents and siblings who have had a child/sibling die, watched over Elisabeth like a mother hen. Elisabeth's son was also close at hand to help his mother.

One Last Visit

Even after her strokes, Elisabeth could still talk on the phone and we talked often. One of triplets, she insisted that she was going to Switzerland to celebrate her seventy-fifth birthday with her sisters. I did not believe she would survive the trip to Switzerland and home again to Scottsdale, so I decided to visit Elisabeth before she left. Izetta Smith wanted desperately to go with me and I wanted her company, so we flew from Portland to Scottsdale, rented a car, and drove to Elisabeth's desert home. We arrived just two days before Elisabeth was to leave for Switzerland.

When Izetta and I were settled in our Scottsdale hotel, I called Elisabeth to see when would be a good time to come the next morning. She asked us to come around 10:00 a.m. The next day I called again to see if there was anything we could bring her. Elisabeth asked for several items, so we stopped at a grocery store on the way. When we arrived, we knocked and she called to us to come in. Elisabeth was in a hospital bed in the living room. She was so glad to see us and in her typical manner, she started telling us what she needed us to do. "First, help me to the bathroom so I can brush my teeth. God, that vould feel so good."

After Izetta and I helped her do all the things she needed, we asked her what she might want to eat. There were several, days-old chocolate cakes, gifts from visitors who often brought her rich desserts. Unfortunately, previous visitors had not taken the time to clean up, so the kitchen counter was full of dirty dishes. We asked Elisabeth what she would like to eat. "Vhat I really vant is some—umm, guacamole. Yes, guacamole! Can you make me some?" We told her that we could but Izetta would need to buy the needed ingredients at a nearby grocery store.

While she was gone, I asked Elisabeth what I could fix for her in the meantime. "Do you know how to make a poached egg?" I assured her I did. I went to the adjoining kitchen, found the eggs and a shallow pan and put water in it. I had the pan on the stove bringing the water to a boil when she called to me, "Put some 'winegar' in the vater and the vhites von't get stringy." I told her I had already put in salt, which did the same thing. I even found an English muffin in the refrigerator on which to put the eggs. When I served her this humble meal, Elisabeth exclaimed, "This is a feast."

Bev Chappell at the entrance to Elisabeth Kübler-Ross' home in Arizona.

IZETTA SMITH

While Izetta was gone, Elisabeth asked to see my manuscript, which I had brought along just in case she might be up to seeing at least a part of it. Elisabeth had encouraged me to write a book about The Dougy Center. She read the chapter about Dougy and an early draft of my introduction. She made a comment about one of the things that I had written regarding someone dying alone. She suggested I change that, saying with complete confidence: "*No one ever dies alone.*" Then, with a big smile, she said, "I like it." Afterwards, I gave her a Rose Quartz heart in a black velvet pouch. Elisabeth told me several times how special it was. I was pleased.

When Izetta returned with the avocado and tomato, she made Elisabeth her guacamole. Elisabeth ate as if she were starved. Izetta and I planned to be there for half an hour to an hour at the most, but every time we told Elisabeth we felt she was getting tired and we should leave, she told us, "Sit down right there," pointing to the chairs by her bedside. She wasn't ready for us to leave. While there, Elisabeth wanted to share a very personal audiotape she and a friend had made about Elisabeth's dying and being ready for that transition. By day's end, our visit lasted more than eight hours.

Before we left, Izetta and I made certain that Elisabeth had all kinds of things on her bedside table to eat and drink. We gave her hugs and kisses, and wished her well on her trip to Switzerland. She assured us once again that she would make it for her seventy-fifth birthday celebration on July 8, 2004. It was hard to leave Elisabeth there alone, even though that was normal for her. On our trip back to the hotel, Izetta and I shed tears of joy for the gift of being able to see Elisabeth one more time. There were tears of sadness, too, knowing we would never see her alive again. We did know we would feel her presence always, especially every time we needed her advice or wanted to share a joy with her. Elisabeth would be here with us always—she promised!

Elisabeth did make it to Switzerland and she took her son, daughter, and granddaughter with her to show them where she grew up and where she had met their dad. She had a great time visiting with her sisters. I heard from Elisabeth one last time in early August 2004. She called and thanked us for coming to see her. Elisabeth also told me she was ready to go now, and she reassured me that when she saw Allan, who had died in 1993, she would give him a hug for me and give him my love. I am betting she did. Elisabeth's death came only four days before the anniversary of Allan's death. Her gravestone includes the inscription, "Graduated to 'dance in the galaxies' on August 24, 2004."

Elisabeth and Emanuel with their children, Barbara and Ken, 1984.

Elisabeth was a great lady who believed in me and knew before I did that I was going to begin a children's grief support program. She had far more faith in me than I had in myself. The Dougy Center became a reality because of Elisabeth and my husband's faith. Elisabeth continued as my mentor and friend from that first step. To this day, she remains my inspiration in spirit.

"What is life and what is death and
why do little children have to die?
Why aren't there any books for children
about dying? If you are old enough to die,
you are old enough to read about it."

DOUG TURNO

CHAPTER THREE

Doug Turno

The Dougy Center for Grieving Children is a tribute to a boy who knew about suffering and fear with the rare insight of a child. He also knew that both could be met with love, understanding, and the joy of life. Doug Turno had a profound message to share about life and love. I consider him one of my greatest inspirations in my work with children. Everyone who met Doug, who we affectionately called Dougy, fell in love with him and was touched by his message.

Dougy was nine years old when he wrote to Dr. Elisabeth Kübler-Ross. Dougy had an inoperable brain tumor and he wanted to know more about dying and death. He asked Elisabeth, "Why aren't there any books for children about dying? If you are old enough to die, you are old enough to read about it." Dr. Ross responded by writing for Dougy his very own book entitled *A Letter to a Child with Cancer from Elisabeth Kübler-Ross.* Later it would be affectionately referred to as *The Dougy Letter.* (See page 94.) Dougy especially liked the last page in the booklet, which read:

> When we have done all the work we were sent to earth to do—we are allowed to shed our body—which imprisons our soul like a cocoon encloses the future butterfly—
>
> —and when the time is right we can let go of it and we will be free of pain, free of fears and worries—free as a very beautiful butterfly, returning home to God which is a place where we are never alone—where we continue to grow and sing and dance, where we are with those we loved (who shed their cocoons earlier) and we are surrounded with more love than we can ever imagine!

The cover of Elisabeth's book that she wrote for Dougy.

Getting to Know Dougy

Dougy was thirteen years old and had been fighting cancer for the past four years. He was traveling to Oregon for a breakthrough cancer therapy. He had been accepted for the treatment as part of cancer research being done at The University of Oregon Health Sciences Center in Portland. Dougy had surgery for a brain tumor in November 1977 followed by radiation therapy. He received more cancer treatment in 1979, but had since developed two new brain tumors, one of which bled, causing Dougy to go into a coma. The treatment in Oregon would hopefully destroy Dougy's tumors and extend his life a few more years. In August 1981, Elisabeth wrote to me about Dougy.

> Dougy is coming to Portland for new research on brain tumors. He is a sweetie pie. You will love him. I told his family you would meet them at the airport and take good care of them. Give your wonderful husband a hug for me.
>
> *—Tons of love, Elisabeth*

Dougy and his parents arrived in Portland on August 15, 1981 and I met them at the airport. After many tiring hours of traveling from his home in Aiken, South Carolina to Portland, Oregon, Dougy arrived with a high fever and feeling very ill. He slowly walked off the plane clutching his Garfield pillow. Dougy asked for a wheelchair even though he really didn't want to admit he needed one. When I greeted him and introduced myself, he thanked me for coming to get him and his parents. His contagious smile overshadowed his fever and the pain.

Immediately I could see that Dougy's friendly and loving presence seemed to touch everyone. Even the Skycap who loaded their luggage into my car was so touched by Dougy that he later visited him several times in the hospital before he would head for his swing-shift job at the airport. I would soon learn that many others who crossed paths with Dougy during his month in Portland would also fall in love with him. It was obvious from my first meeting with Dougy that he had the maturity and wisdom of a wise old man, and although desperately ill, he always had a smile and compassion for his fellow human beings.

Dougy and Bev in Portland September 1981. Dougy's puffy face was the result of steroids.

Dougy also had a ready sense of humor and enjoyed a subtle joke, almost always unexpected. In retrospect, perhaps much of his sense of humor was his way to help ease the adults around him who were uncomfortable in the presence of a dying child. One day my husband went with me to visit Doug in the hospital. Dougy broke the ice in those awkward moments when they first met. He held up a small black and white, spotted stuffed dog with a child's wrist watch around its middle. The watch no longer fit around Dougy's puffy wrist.

He asked Allan, "Do you know what this is?"

Allan replied, "A Dalmation?"

"No!"

"A stuffed toy dog?"

Doug giggled another "No!"

Then Allan said, "I give up! What is it?"

Doug grinned from ear to ear as he teased, "It's a watch dog."

Throughout my time of knowing Dougy, I was continually impressed with how he reached out to other children who were also in the late stages of their life-threatening illnesses. As gravely ill as he was, Dougy kept saying, "I can go to the hospitals and tell other kids not to be afraid to die!" He had asked Elisabeth to send him as many copies of *The Dougy Letter* as she could; and when he was able, he visited the other patients on the cancer ward in his wheelchair and gave those he visited one of Elisabeth's booklets.

One of my lasting memories of Dougy is the story about how he reached out to Johnny. He was a bit younger than Dougy and his mother had sent Johnny to the hospital in a taxi. His mom had just gone through a bitter divorce, and as she would later explain, "I could not handle another loss." Johnny was in immense pain and so afraid when he arrived at the hospital. The nurses gave Johnny a shot for pain and oxygen to help him breathe more easily. Then they moved Johnny's bed next to the nurses' station area so he would not be alone. His bed was directly outside Dougy's room. For some time, Dougy watched what was going on just outside his door. Knowing only what the nurse had told his mom about Johnny's situation, Dougy felt compelled to do something to lessen this boy's fear and aloneness.

At that time, Dougy suffered from loss of balance and he was unable to walk without help. His brain tumor was causing double vision and he was also in great pain. Despite his medical condition, Dougy eased himself out of his bed and into his nearby wheelchair. With great determination, he guided his wheelchair around the bed, suitcases, chairs, and other obstacles in his hospital room so he could reach a shelf in the corner. Many stuffed animals, gifts from his visitors, congregated in that special corner. Dougy would always have a broad grin when he talked about imagining these animals whispering among themselves about what they sensed was happening around them. Also on that shelf was a collection of gumdrops, gifts from visitors who knew how much Dougy loved gumdrops. And there were roses, one of Dougy's favorite flowers. He pulled himself to his feet and stood long enough to collect a bag of gumdrops and one of his prized stuffed animals. Dropping back into his wheelchair, Dougy guided himself out of his room and into the hallway next to Johnny's bedside.

At first, the two boys looked at each other in silence. Then Dougy spoke. "I brought you one of my stuffed friends to keep you company. And maybe when you are feeling a little better you would like some gumdrops." Johnny reached out to receive the gumdrops and the stuffed animal. He smiled, but there wasn't any conversation. Johnny was so ill that a smile was the only way he could respond. And Dougy was so sick, too, he understood. The next morning Dougy insisted on going to the gift shop before heading to his radiation therapy. He wanted to buy with his own money a stuffed animal for Johnny to keep.

Johnny's aunt came to visit him the next day and frequently from then on. Soon she was able to convince Johnny's mother that she needed to be at the hospital with Johnny before he died. When Johnny's illness became more serious his father had disappeared. Johnny's mom did not think she was able to handle her ex-husband's abrupt leaving along with what she knew would be Johnny's impending death. However, the mom was finally able to spend some quality time with her son. Johnny was too ill for much conversation, but she sat beside him, held his hand, and talked to him—and on occasion quietly sang to him.

This story exemplifies what I most remember about Dougy—he lived fully even in his dying. Dougy reached out to others who also were dying, to the hospital staff who cared for him, to the chaplains who visited him, and to the parents of other children who were suffering their own losses. Dougy certainly reached out to my husband and me. In the month that Dougy was in Portland, the profoundness of his life touched more people than can be imagined, from restaurant owners to Pacific Bell Telephone employees to bookstore clerks, and many others he met along his path. Dougy knew he was on a journey, and he knew *Who* held his hand on that journey.

Dougy's Final Months

Doctors had inserted a tube into the artery at the top of Dougy's leg and threaded the tube into his neck. They injected drugs to penetrate the brain's blood barrier with the hope that this would destroy Dougy's tumors. The experimental therapy did not work. The tumor was in a vital part of his brain that controlled respiration and heart function. Anything added to the brain, specifically the chemotherapy solution, would put pressure on that area of his brain and kill him immediately. Dougy's physician recommended that he and his family return home immediately while Dougy was still conscious and able to sit up on the airplane. So, exactly a month after arriving in Portland, Doug flew home to South Carolina with his mom and his sister. His dad had left earlier to return to work.

On December 5, 1981, less than three months after arriving home, Dougy got his wish: "A new life for Christmas." Even at thirteen years old he was not afraid to die, he only needed to be certain that his family could make it when he did let go.

Dougy's last Christmas photo with his siblings shortly before he died. From left, Terri, Danny, David, Derek, Don, and Megan.

Years later, Dougy's sister, Megan, shared a poem she had written in May 1981, about six months before Dougy died. I had grown to love Megan whom I had met during Dougy's stay in Portland. At the time, Megan was twenty-three years old. She was concerned for her little brother who was ill and not expected to get better. Dougy had six siblings, but he had a particularly close-knit relationship with Megan, even though she was ten years older than Dougy. Megan wrote:

> Do you ever cry and not know why?
>> A song, a picture, a memory of some special time and place?
> Do you ever hurt way deep inside?
>> A dark, vast emptiness?
> Do you ever wish that it were all through
>> But then call back those words?
> Do you long to hold someone you love
>> As if your arms could stop the hurt, the pain, the sorrow?
> Yet, during all this, treasure those golden moments
>> Brought only through such tears, such pain,
>>> Such love?
>>>> I do.
>
> —Megan Turno

In August 1982, less than a year after Dougy's death, I sat on a piece of driftwood on the Oregon coast, my heart still full with memories of Dougy and his brief, yet powerful life. As I watched the wind-roughened Pacific Ocean pound the shore, I pondered the possibility of a support program for young people facing death. I also thought about their siblings facing that loss. I imagined a place where teens and younger children in grief could share their feelings. They would see, share, and support other children who also suffered loss and pain. *It would be called The Dougy Center*, I thought. *What better acknowledgment for a young boy who had touched so many peoples' hearts?*

CHAPTER FOUR

Unmet Grief

L ong before I had a plan for creating a center for grieving children, I often watched the dynamics of families dealing with death and grief, and the unfolding of painful family drama because of unmet grief. This was the fallout when a grieving child or an entire family did not have the information or the psychological tools to express their grief and find healing. Their grief needs went unmet.

The first family that opened my eyes to the effects of unmet grief was an average family that we had been friends with since the 1960s. My experiences with this family led the way to what became my journey to discovering more about dying, death, and grief—especially concerning children. The Edwards family included the father, James; the mother, Janice; the older sister, Melissa; and the younger brother, Jimmy Paul. The children had been my husband's patients when they lived in Portland. Later, when they moved to the Oregon coast, we stayed at their motel while we vacationed. While there, my husband and I, as well as our children, were aware of the upsetting relationships going on within the family. Years later, I began recognizing these same family dynamics in other families where grief was left unresolved.

A Death in the Family

James Edwards ran his own shoe repair business in Portland. James' brothers had shoe repair shops, too, under the family name. In 1958, when Melissa was six and Jimmy Paul four, a new baby joined the family. Susie was adorable and the light of everyone's life. Soon after her birth, Susie began to look jaundiced, and Allan, as her pediatrician, diagnosed Susie with biliary atresia, which Allan described as a congenital absence of the bile duct. Years later doctors learned to remedy this condition with a liver transplant, but that was unheard of in the late 1950s. The prognosis was almost always an early death, but the time allotted varied.

When Janice had Susie with her in her stroller while shopping, people would stop and tell her, "Your baby doesn't look well. Do you ever take her to see the doctor?" Janice's immediate reply was always, "We live on his doorstep." Susie often hemorrhaged and they would rush her to the hospital where my husband would meet them. This happened more and more often as the disease progressed.

One night in October 1960 they rushed Susie to the hospital, again because of hemorrhaging. Before they left home, Janice grabbed all of Susie's blood stained bedding, rolled it up, and threw it in the basement so Melissa and Jimmy Paul would not see it. The parents tried to hide Susie's illness from their other children. Once again, the grandmother came over and stayed with the older kids. Once Susie was resting quietly at the hospital, Janice and James returned home so that Grandmother could leave. James returned to the hospital around 4:45 that morning to see how Susie was doing. While he sat at her bedside a train whistle blew in the distance. Susie opened her eyes and said softly with the recognition of a two-and-a-half-year old, "Choo Choo." Shortly after that she closed her eyes and died.

A few weeks after Susie's death, I had the opportunity to talk with Janice. She told me that on the day of the funeral Melissa and Jimmy Paul were sent off to school as if it were an ordinary day. None of the adults told the children about the funeral in an effort to protect them. No one explained to Melissa and Jimmy Paul the seriousness of Susie's illness, or why she had died. The children knew she had been in and out of the hospital often and were aware that she was ill, but Susie had always come home. After her death, Melissa and Jimmy Paul were told that Susie had gone to heaven.

James could not tolerate being in their home without Susie and often drove to the Oregon coast to escape the emptiness. Before long, he bought a small group of apartments overlooking the Pacific Ocean. He moved the family to one of the apartments and rented out the other units as motel rooms. This was a complete shift from the shoe repair business. Things went well and in no time he built a new motel with twenty units. Around this time our family began taking our vacations at their new motel overlooking the ocean. Our two children were of comparable ages to their two children and they all became playmates when we went to the coast.

For several years the motel business kept James busy enough to not have to think too much about the death of his daughter. In 1964, they added a restaurant which burned down a year and a half later and had to be rebuilt. Several years later they built thirty-five more units for a total of fifty-five motel units. Through all of this, Melissa and Jimmy Paul fought constantly, James drank, and Janice withdrew into her own world to escape. While still living in Portland, Janice drove to the cemetery every other day. After the move to the coast, Janice helped James to some extent, but was there primarily as a full time mother.

A Mix of Joy and Grief

In 1965, a little more than five years after Susie's death, Janice had another baby. During her pregnancy, Janice thought she was carrying a boy and that pleased all of them. But she gave birth to a girl and let out a scream when the doctor told her. The doctor thought Janice was angry, but her scream was one of delight. She was thrilled! They named their new daughter Suzanne—never to be called Susie!

This new baby was not, and never would be, their precious child who died. The older children were disappointed that it was not the boy they had expected, but seemed okay with Suzanne for about two years. I suspect they were afraid to get too close to her for fear she would die, too. Either that, or they decided she did not measure up to the baby sister they had lost. Whatever the reason, Melissa and Jimmy Paul began being very mean to Suzanne. Not only was Suzanne treated badly by her older siblings, her parents began to detach from Suzanne, realizing she would never be their little girl who had died. Sadly, the family never cherished Suzanne.

When Suzanne was eighteen months old, Janice had another child, a boy named Brice. Brice became the darling of the family, and with his sweet disposition, he got along with everyone. It was special for little Suzanne to have this extremely close relationship with Brice, but still her relationship with the rest of the family was never good while growing up. The older children were close to Brice, but never to Suzanne.

On occasion, when we were staying at their motel, our daughter, Kathy, would come to our unit and throw herself across the bed and sob because Jimmy Paul and Melissa were being so mean to Suzanne. Between sobs Kathy would say, "It's not just once in a while. It is all the time! They push her down, they hide from her and take her things and run away." As the children got older, this mean-spirited treatment continued endlessly.

Along with all the other things that were going on in the family, Jimmy Paul was diagnosed with juvenile diabetes at age eight. The entire family seemed to take this in their stride and did what they could to handle each new situation the best they knew how. When Brice was twelve, he was diagnosed with cerebral palsy, but as the scoliosis (curvature) of his spine worsened, that diagnosis was questioned. As he became less and less able to do things or to stand up straight, the doctors did more tests. Brice was put in a body brace.

By the time Brice was in a wheelchair, the doctors were still uncertain of the diagnosis. He had a battery of tests, X-rays, MRIs and CT scans to get to the bottom of what was really going on in his body. The final diagnosis was spino-cerebellar degeneration, which was a collection of degenerative nerve diseases affecting peripheral nerves, an inherited condition.

When Janice heard the diagnosis, she asked what the prognosis might be. The unfeeling physician replied, "Prognosis? Well, death, naturally! They never live beyond the age of nineteen." Brice overheard the conversation, but did not discuss the information with his parents. A short time after hearing this diagnosis conversation, Brice attempted suicide by taking an entire bottle of Phenobarbital, which had been prescribed for him earlier. Brice went through his high school years in a wheelchair.

At this time in the life of the Edwards family, James had stopped drinking; however, he ended up having a nervous breakdown. In 1979, he told Janice that he didn't want to be married anymore. She was brokenhearted, but they separated and she moved back to Portland with the children. Janice worked as a switchboard operator at a local high school district office, and later as an assistant in an attorney's office. They had been divorced for nine months when one day James came to see Janice and the children. He told her he wanted to be married again. They remarried, and she and the children moved back to the coast.

Unmet Grief in the Teen and Adult Years

By this time, and with all the things that had happened within the family, the older children, Melissa and Jimmy Paul, now called JP, had both entered crisis mode and were acting out their emotions in all kinds of self-destructive ways. They both began drinking when they were about fourteen years old; not just an occasional drink, but drinking to excess. And the drinking got them both into trouble. JP was cited for multiple Driving Under the Influence of Intoxicants (DUII) infractions. He spent time in jail, and had his license suspended. Their drinking problems led to painful adult years and shattered lives.

Brice somehow seemed able to roll with the punches, so to speak, even though he was not able to do most of the things teens take for granted. At one point in the 1970s when I was learning about children and spontaneous drawings, I asked Brice to draw some pictures. His drawings reflected bleakness, hopelessness and despair. In one drawing, it looks as if a tree is waving good-bye. (Brice's drawings are on pages 89 to 93.)

Despite Brice's lack of independence, his disposition was mellow and sweet. In his electric wheelchair with an orange flag on a pole waving high above, he navigated the shoulder of the road to the next town south of where they lived. This wasn't easy on his parents, but they knew how important it was for Brice to have as much independence as possible. He enjoyed these outings.

As time went on, Brice became less mobile and he was unable to sit comfortably in his wheelchair. Often, Brice crawled on the floor to move across the room. In time he needed to be carried whenever he wanted to move from one place to another. James hurt his back and was no longer able to carry Brice, and he was too heavy for Janice. Brice had to be placed in a care center, where he remained for two-and-one-half years until his death in August 1997 at age thirty-one.

Brice's death was one more difficult loss for a family that had continued to experience loss after loss. The family visited Brice daily in the care center, and unlike at the time of Susie's death, all of the siblings attended his funeral.

Many Children, Many Lessons

In 1999, James and Janice sold the motel and the restaurant that they had worked so hard to build and retired to an area close by. All of their children lived in the area and some of the children continued to work at the motel for a time.

Suzanne was married for less than three years when her husband died of a heart attack. They had a little girl who was two years old when her dad died. In spite of all the difficult mean things that happened to Suzanne while she was growing up, her mother Janice says Suzanne is the most loving and giving of all of the children—and very patient with the rest of her family.

Melissa, who is in her fourth marriage, is happy now. JP never married. His diabetes is beginning to take its toll on his health. James died suddenly of a cardiac arrest while driving the car.

Over many years, this family showed me the long-term effects of what unmet grief was all about within a family. While I watched how they dealt, or did not deal, with all of the deaths and grief that came their way, I began to realize that children found it difficult to talk to grieving parents and parents seemed unable to share their feelings with their children in an effort to protect them. Over the years I wondered: *Would it help if the children had other children in similar situations to talk to? Would that make a difference?*

It took many more years of watching the dynamics of families such as this one to finally realize something needed to be done about what I was witnessing. The children in many different families kept teaching me in a variety of situations until I could no longer ignore the need for a special place for grieving children.

CHAPTER FIVE

A Toddler's Death

Some seven years before the first support group took place at The Dougy Center, I worked with a family in an official capacity as an advocate for the first time. I had met Elisabeth Kübler-Ross the year before, and I was taking death and grieving workshops as well as teaching classes. I knew this would be my passion and my life's work, now that my children were grown.

In October 1975, I got a call came from Northeast Children's Services. "Do you work with families where someone has a life-threatening illness?" the social worker asked.

"Yes," I replied.

"We have a black family with a single mom who is just recovering from a hysterectomy and having many complications. She has two older daughters, ten and twelve, and a ten-month-old baby who has leukemia. He is not doing well. They need an advocate, someone to talk to, someone who is sensitive to their needs and will truly care about them and their situation. Would you be interested in seeing them?"

"Sure, I'll be happy to visit them and see if there is anything I can do to help," I offered. The social worker gave me their address and phone number, and I gave them a call. We juggled our calendar dates and finally settled on a day and time when I could come visit them.

The day arrived and I drove to their home in a modest apartment complex in north Portland. Driving around the area I finally spotted their apartment number and pulled into a parking space in front of their door. I took a deep breath and gave a silent prayer that I could give them some degree of support and caring. Before getting out of the car, I noticed the curtains in the apartment moved and partially hidden children's faces peered out the window.

Florence, the mom, opened the door and greeted me. It was obvious that she was skeptical about this white woman at her door. Years later after we had become good friends, Florence shared her first thoughts upon seeing me: *"Who is this rich, got rocks woman and what does she think she can do to make things better around here?"*

When I first arrived, our conversation was stiff and tense, but in time we both began to relax a bit. She wanted to know if anyone in my family had a life-threatening illness. I shared that our daughter, Kathy, had recently been diagnosed with an extremely rare, incurable, life-threatening illness that few physicians had even heard of. In addition, Kathy had left home only six weeks after the diagnosis to teach ice skating in Seattle. Once I had shared this story about myself, Florence's entire countenance changed. She wanted to know how my husband and I could possibly let our daughter leave home where we could keep our eye on her and take care of her. I had to admit that was the most difficult thing I had to do since Kathy's birth twenty years earlier.

The longer we chatted, the softer and more communicative Florence became. We had been talking for quite a while when a whimper came from a back room. Her younger daughter, Keesha, said, "The baby is awake. Should I change him?" Florence told her to go ahead and then bring her little brother out because he needed another dose of his medicine. When Keesha brought out little James, he immediately climbed into my lap and began playing with my keys. Both girls were dumbfounded that their baby brother had accepted me so readily. In turn, the girls began to warm up to me.

We all talked for quite a while, growing more at ease with each other. When it was time for me to leave, I asked, "Is there anything you need me to do? I would like to be of help." In unison they responded, "Will you come back to see us?"

I gave Florence my phone number and told her that if ever she needed to talk or wanted my assistance in any way to please give me a call. Then she asked me, "What time is too late?" I assured her that no time was too late. She could call any time of the day or night. Florence stood there in disbelief. Since my husband was a pediatrician, I was used to the phone ringing in our home at all hours during the night, so this would not be unusual. I knew Allan would understand.

I made frequent visits, oftentimes weekly. Once when James was feeling a bit better we went to a park so Florence's girls could play. They needed to be children rather than second mommies. As we got to know each other, we both relaxed. She told me she felt blessed that James had so completely bonded with me. She thought part of it was because I did not inflict any hurtful medical procedures, which was usually the case when James was at the hospital.

James' illness ran a rugged course and he had frequent treatments and many hospitalizations. The medical staff kept Florence in another room during James' spinal taps, bone marrow tests, and intravenous infusions of medications. It tore her apart hearing him scream and not being allowed in the room where she could attempt to comfort her son. The girls sobbed while they listened to their little brother scream. Florence had to hold and comfort her daughters as her tears mingled with theirs. If James had to stay overnight at the hospital, Florence stayed in the room with him while a family member would stay with the girls.

My husband met the family and they loved him. They asked Allan medical questions that they did not feel comfortable asking James' doctors. Sometimes, they had questions about James' treatment in between visits to see his doctors.

Staying close by this family's side, I witnessed James' ongoing hospital stays where he took the horrible tasting chemotherapy syrup. He was one very sick little fellow without a remission for months. Then in March, five months after I first met the family, James went into his first and only short remission from his debilitating leukemia. The weather was unusually warm and James was able to run in the park and experience childhood things he had never been able to do before. Florence and the girls were so happy to see little James in the best health he had ever experienced.

One night during this time, a dream awakened me. In this dream James had died in June on my birthday. I thought: *This doesn't make sense. He is doing so well right now.* It was March and difficult to imagine everything falling apart so quickly for James.

A Downward Spiral

The remission was short-lived, and by mid-April James' leukemia reared its ugly head more intensely than ever. Nothing medicine offered could bring him back to another remission. James continued to spiral downward, growing sicker each day. The family was devastated. The girls could hardly go to school and when they did, they could not keep their minds on their studies. James spent most of his time in the hospital now and Florence was constantly at his side. Florence's mother took care of the girls and often brought them to the hospital after school to spend time with their mother and brother. By June, James' condition hit bottom, but the family still held on to hope.

James' hospital room adjoined an examination room. A thin wall with a large window separated the two rooms. The doctors would take James into this room for treatments, closing the window curtains so that Florence could not see what they were doing to her precious baby, who by then was not quite eighteen months old. But she could still hear his heart-wrenching screams. One day Florence decided she could no longer handle it by herself. She called me. "Could you please come to the hospital and be with me? They have James in the treatment room and he is screaming and I can't take it any longer." She paused, and then added, "I am sorry to ask you to come all the way up here, but if you have time, I would like to have you be here with me." I told her I would come right away.

When I arrived, I found Florence sitting in the rocking chair with her Bible opened on her lap. Tears streamed down her face. When she looked up and saw me she gasped, "You came!" While I held her in my arms she sobbed, "Others have told me they would come, but they never did." Together we held one another as we listened to the screaming. In our hearts, we screamed too, as we silently cried.

When the nurse brought James back to his room, she told us the doctor would be in to talk to us. Then she added, "But what he has to say is not going to be encouraging." Florence held James who was still sobbing. If love could have healed him, she certainly had enough to make him well.

When the doctor came into the room, he told Florence there was not much else they could do to help James. The doctor felt they had exhausted all that current medicine had to offer. He ended by saying,

"He will probably not live much longer." As the doctor walked out of the room, Florence held James close and I embraced them both as we all quietly wept, little James still shaking with soft sobs. I knew there was nothing to say at a time like this. Just being there seemed to be important. Many weeks later, Florence confirmed that my presence had made it much easier for her to bear the news. Florence and James were my teachers in learning how to be with someone facing this kind of difficult news.

When there was an opportunity, I left the hospital room for a few minutes and called my husband to tell him what had just happened. Allan was shocked that the doctor had given Florence this dreadful news and then just walked out of the room. Allan said he would come to the hospital as soon as he finished with patients. When he arrived, he gave Florence a hug and then went to find the doctor who had spoken to her. On returning, Allan explained to us the doctors' findings after that long afternoon with James in the examination room. The chemo drugs they had been using were no longer effective, in fact they were doing more damage than good, and there was nothing else to try. All the doctors could offer was to keep James as comfortable as possible.

The doctor who delivered the bad news admitted to Allan that he could not face the mother because he not only felt like a failure, but that was also what parents considered him when nothing else could be done for their child. When the doctor admitted this, my husband told him, "Tender loving care given to the mother is probably the best help for you, and it is definitely the best that you can give a mother at a time like this. She needs to know that you care, that you didn't just walk away."

Florence constantly sat at James' bedside or held him for most of the final six days. Her family kept bringing her clean clothes, food she didn't eat, and supportive visits. In the final three days, James was in so much pain he could not tolerate being held. The night before his death, Florence went out to the nurses' desk to call home and collapsed on the floor, unconscious. Her family insisted she come home for the night. Florence's mother stayed at the hospital and was with James when he died.

Florence was devastated and felt so guilty for not being with James when he died. Repeatedly, she told me James was such a fighter that she knew he would have lived longer had she been there. I told her that I had seen many children, and adults, too, who seemed to wait for their loved ones to leave, if only for a cup of coffee or to use the bathroom. Once family members were gone, then the dying individual could let go and die. It was as if the presence of loved ones prevented the dying from happening. As we talked, Florence and I held each other. I had never felt someone else's pain flow so severely through me. Added to my own pain, it felt all but unbearable.

Florence's mother took her wilted and sagging daughter and her two granddaughters home. I, too, left for home. Elisabeth Kübler-Ross, my mentor, had not warned me that I would feel each loss as if it were my own. Nor did she warn me that I would have to do my own grieving with each loss.

A Child's Funeral

I didn't hear from Florence for two days after James' death and then she called to make certain that I had seen the funeral notice in the newspaper and would be coming. She read to me something she had written for her son that she planned to read at the funeral. She wanted to know if I thought it was okay. It touched me deeply.

The church was crowded. I noted that the African-American families in attendance did not leave their children home in an attempt to protect them from this "horrible thing called death." Parents were there with their small children—from babes in arms to toddlers to pre-schoolers, and older children, as well. The casket was open and situated in the middle of the aisle at the front of the church. This precious baby was so beautiful. No longer in pain, James' face looked so peaceful. In the front pew to the left of the middle aisle sat six young pallbearers about eight to eleven years old. All were dressed in white suits, with white shoes, socks, and gloves. They sat quietly, as if the sight of death and grief was familiar.

After the service, the minister invited people to come forward for the viewing. Families moved toward James' open casket. Parents lifted small children to see James and many children pulled themselves up to peer over the edge of the casket. Some of the children put a stuffed animal into the casket and some leaned down to kiss James. It amazed me how comfortable these little ones were with the entire funeral experience. It was obvious they had done this before. The response from James' family and the community was a great lesson for me, coming from a cultural background that was so often uncomfortable with death and grief.

At the cemetery, all the families gathered with Florence and her family. After a short service, the casket was lowered into the ground. Almost everyone threw a handful of dirt onto the casket. Each of James' family members also threw in a single flower. As I drove home that day, I thought, *This has been another life-learning journey that I will never forget.*

CHAPTER SIX

"Where's My Mommy? Where's My Daddy?"

"Pilot to tower: Mayday! Mayday! We're goin' down!"

It was December 28, 1978, and in Northeast Portland there was a deafening sound of a plane rapidly falling, then trees thundering to the ground as a United DC-8 crashed into two vacant houses and a grove of trees. The plane had apparently run out of fuel while circling the Portland International Airport in an attempt to land and had to make an emergency landing five miles from the airport.

The newspaper headline the next day read:

> United DC-8 crashes at East Burnside,
> 157th; 10 killed, 176 survive, 18 still hospitalized.

And farther down the page in smaller print, the tagline read:

> Girl, 3, lone survivor in family of 5

The Oregonian article reported:

> Elizabeth Andor (Lisa) was in serious but stable condition Friday at a local hospital after county officials secured a temporary wardship for the hospital to allow treatment of her injuries.
>
> Dead are her father, Gabor, believed to be in his late thirties, his wife, Rosina, and two daughters, Gabriella, 2, and Rosina, 1, who had celebrated her first birthday on Christmas Eve.
>
> The surviving child is Elizabeth, 3, who suffered a fractured right leg and head injuries after she was trapped between two seats near the place where the plane's cabin broke open in the

crash. She was pulled from the wreckage by two Multnomah County sheriff's deputies.

From the moment Lisa entered the hospital, Portland Adventist Hospital became her legal guardian because there was no family present to make decisions on her behalf. She immediately needed surgery for a badly fractured leg. The doctors put her leg in traction to keep it elevated and stretched so it would heal. Lisa was in a room by herself so she would not overhear any conversations about the crash or the death of her family members. Every time anyone came into the room, Lisa asked, "Where's my mommy, where's my daddy? Where are my sisters, Gabby and Rosie?"

Telling Lisa the Truth

Lisa's grandfather and uncle traveled from Chicago to represent the family. They insisted that no one tell Lisa that her family had died in the crash. The Director of the Department of Social Work, Ed Cochrane, visited Lisa and he was met with the same questions every time he saw her. Ed had trained for many death and grief issues, but he wanted some assistance with this, so he called me. Ed told me how frustrating this situation was for the little girl and for him. He asked, "Would you come over to the hospital so we might visit Lisa together?"

When I first met this delightful three year old, she told us, "I'm a big girl. I haven't wet the bed one time!" And then she began the constant questions, "Where are my mommy and daddy?" Ed and I looked at each other. Her grandfather and uncle watched us like hawks. I told Lisa that we would tell her as soon as we found out what happened for sure. I thought to myself: *At least we had not lied to her and I think she knows that.*

On some level, Lisa knew that her family was gone and not in some other hospital recovering. Lisa also knew that what she was being told was not true, so every time someone different came into her room—the nurse, doctor or a visitor—Lisa asked about her family. When these questions went on for a week and the grandfather and uncle continued to withhold the truth, Ed and I could no longer stand it. We tried to talk to the family members to no avail. In their thinking, they were doing the best thing for this three year-old child. We tried to convince them that Lisa already knew. For more years than imaginable, adults have felt the need to protect children from knowing about, or being a part of, a death situation. I tried to explain that often the things children imagine are far worse than hearing the truth.

With each passing day Lisa was getting more and more distressed. Finally, Ed told the grandfather and uncle that we were going to tell Lisa the truth the next day whether they approved or not. "She needs to know the truth," we insisted. They stood firmly opposed.

The following day, more than a week after the plane crash, we arrived at Lisa's hospital room door with two Multnomah County deputies. They were ready to do whatever might be necessary so we could talk to Lisa. Fortunately, the deputies did not have to do anything. Both the grandfather and the uncle left the room quickly, but before they got to the door the uncle shouted, "Lisa, Mommy and Daddy and your sisters are dead! They died when the plane crashed! You won't ever see them anymore." Then they ran down the hall leaving us to pick up the pieces. With searching eyes Lisa looked up at us begging for some answers.

At first we asked Lisa, "Do you know where your family is?" She responded that she heard people in the hallway say they died when the plane fell out of the sky, but she wasn't sure what "died" meant. We explained the best way we could to a three year old. We told her that when someone dies they can no longer eat or breathe or go to the bathroom. They cannot move or think or even give her a hug anymore. We asked her if she had ever seen a dead bird or squirrel. She had, and we thought Lisa finally understood, at least for that moment, that she would not see them again. But for a child under the age of five or six, death is a temporary happening and when the person "has been dead long enough," in a child's way of reasoning, it is time for the dead loved ones to come back or get up and play with them again. She seemed extremely wise for her age and repeated back to us much of what we told her. When Lisa was finished, she asked, "Is that right?"

There were a few tears, but Lisa looked relieved to know the truth. We then asked her who would be the best person to be with her. Lisa's eyes widened and she got a huge smile on her face. "Big John! Can Big John come to see me?" Big John was a neighbor and a good friend of the family. Lisa's mother and John's wife were best friends. Both families lived in Vancouver, Washington. We soon learned that Lisa's parents had appointed John and his wife to be the girls' godparents in case anything should ever happen to them. The legal papers were all written out and signed by both families, but they had not been notarized.

John had gone to the hospital as soon as he heard Lisa was alive, but the relatives would not allow him to see her. At Lisa's request, the hospital, which still had custody, called John and told him Lisa wanted to see him. What a reunion! She was so happy to see John. Lisa hugged and kissed him, and held him close, not wanting Big John to leave her side. All of us who watched this reunion had tears streaming down our cheeks.

Who Gets Lisa?

In the following weeks, whenever the phone rang at the nurses' desk, Lisa would get wide eyed, pull her closed fists up to her chest, and in a deep breath say, "That's Big John calling Lisa." Sometimes it was. Most of the time John was at the hospital with her, much to the grandfather's and uncle's dismay. Several times when John was at the hospital, he met with the social worker, Ed, in his office. On one visit John brought the paperwork with all the signatures appointing him and his wife as the godparents and legal guardians. John wanted to know what to do to make this known. Ed helped him find an attorney to represent John. At the same time Ed warned John that without the paperwork being notarized he might have trouble if the grandparents and aunt and uncle wanted to fight for Lisa's custody. John told Ed the reason her parents moved to this part of the country was to get their children out of Chicago. He shook his head sadly, and said, "That was the reason they wanted us to be their godparents in case anything ever happened. We never dreamed it would be something like this." His eyes brimmed with tears.

Ed stopped in to see Lisa often, as did my husband and I. Allan would visit Lisa each evening when he finished making his hospital rounds. They became good friends. One evening when we were both visiting Lisa, we watched her play with a little toy car. She was running it back and forth across the table that had held her dinner tray. Suddenly she clenched her teeth, pushed down on the car and rolled it severely across the surface so that it flew off the table. Allan picked it up and gave it back to her. She did this over and over again. Repeatedly, Lisa continued to crash the car. We realized it was not merely a game; she was venting her anger. Lisa did not know what "dead" meant, but she did know her family was not with her and it left an emptiness she could not fill, nor could anyone else. Throwing this car on the floor with all her force was the only way this little girl knew to vent her anger, confusion, and emptiness.

When Lisa's grandfather and uncle became aware that John had hired an attorney to fight for custody of Lisa, they became furious and found themselves an attorney, as well. They had thought it was an uncontested situation because they were biological family, but John had the paperwork, though not notarized, that was his case for custody. After an involved and painful court hearing, the court decided the uncle, aunt, and grandparents would be the legal guardians. Lisa was unhappy. She did not know these people. She and her family had been close to John and his family since her birth.

Toward the end of January the doctors took Lisa's leg out of traction. She was put into a cast extending from high on her chest and back, down to her knee on one side, and down to her toes on the other. Lisa was terribly uncomfortable and for the first time since the airplane crash she cried because of pain.

The doctors decided Lisa could leave the hospital the next day. When I visited Lisa that day the nurse told me, "When Dr. Chappell was here on hospital rounds this morning he whispered something to Lisa and she ceased crying and got a big smile on her face. She wouldn't tell anyone what he had told her. That was their secret."

Early the next morning before Lisa left the hospital Allan lifted her, body cast and all, onto a gurney and wheeled her down the hall. Both of them had smiles on their faces. He took Lisa to the nursery window and the nurse held up newborn babies for her to see. Then Allan took some pictures of Lisa and promised to send them to her. That was the last time we saw her.

Considering The Child's Perspective

Again, I experienced a situation where a child was left out of the equation when a death took someone out of his or her life. In this case, it was Lisa's entire family. In addition, she was then uprooted from her neighborhood and friends she knew. I was appalled to see how little was considered from this child's point of view. Lisa's parents had moved to the Pacific Northwest to raise their family in a cleaner, more open environment, but after their death Lisa was taken back to the very place her parents had intentionally left—Chicago.

Repeatedly, I saw that most adults did not consider the child's perspective. At that time, adults did not acknowledge that children did, indeed, grieve. It was not only the families of children who had experienced the death that needed to be educated on the child's behalf, but it was also the professionals who did not believe children grieved. In my experience, the child psychologists, child psychiatrists, Chief of Pediatrics, and Chief of Pediatric Oncology at the medical school had never given children's loss and grief consideration. That was a challenge for me, and for my husband as well, so we decided that we would do something about it.

CHAPTER SEVEN

Loss Compounded by Loss

My grief work with families, one-on-one, prepared me for the work I would one day do at The Dougy Center. Several families affected me tremendously, offering insights, epiphanies, and a growing clarity as to *why* there needed to be a place where grieving children could be with other grieving children and express their feelings. These were not easy paths I walked with families, witnessing up close their pain, confusion, and huge emotional voids that often went unseen, unheard, and aching for years.

Perhaps one of the most painful stories I experienced was that of a young boy whose father died, and the subsequent losses that ensued because of an ongoing custody battle between the step family and Mark's biological mother. Mark's initial grief over his dad's death was soon layered with the pain and grief of losing his family, followed by an abusive biological mother, neglect, a misguided custody judge, and multiple losses. To this day, I am haunted by the multitude of Mark's losses.

Mark's Story

It was Friday, February 29, 1980, and eight-year-old Mark had been home from school all week with a cold. He had improved enough that he could have returned to school, but his parents decided to wait until Monday and let him go with his dad on a business trip to Seattle. Mark was delighted to be asked to accompany his dad, Ben, so off they went, taking Mark's new puppy along for the adventure.

It had been a good day in Seattle. Ben completed his business, and then they enjoyed dinner with friends. Later that evening Ben and Mark left to head home to Portland. Mark fell asleep in the car, curled up with his cuddly warm puppy. What happened after that is not certain, but investigators at the scene of the accident believe something had been making a strange sound on the driver's side of the car so Ben had pulled onto the shoulder of the freeway to check on the noise. It was almost 11:30 p.m. and they were heading south on Interstate 5 near Fort Lewis, Washington.

A traffic-monitoring helicopter was circling above the freeway, a usual occurrence in that area. The pilot had been following an erratically-driven car ever since it had left the grounds at Fort Lewis. Suddenly, the pilot shouted, "Oh, my God! He's drunk! He's going to kill that fellow!" The pilot's reaction was recorded on a tape that was played in court weeks later.

The drunk driver hit Ben and dragged him many yards along the freeway. Immediately, the helicopter pilot called the police and an ambulance. Police flashlights scanning the inside of the car woke Mark just as medics loaded Ben's body into the ambulance. The police told Mark his father had been hurt and they were taking him to the hospital. Mark did not know that his dad had been killed instantly. The police called Mark's stepmother in Portland, who asked the police to take Mark back to the friend's home in Seattle where they had visited earlier.

When Mark returned to Portland on Sunday, family members greeted him with long hugs and rivers of tears. His step-mom, Sally, who had been his mother for nearly four years, put him in a warm bath. While bathing him, she told Mark that his father had died immediately when the car hit him and he probably felt no pain. Sally wrapped Mark in a cozy towel when he got out of the tub and held him while they cried together. As they rocked back and forth, crying, Sally tried to answer Mark's questions and comfort him, even though in intense shock herself.

Marks' birth mother, Doris, arrived that evening, unexpected and unwanted. She had heard the news of Ben's death on television and had come to assess the situation. Doris had left Mark and his father on Christmas day when Mark was two and a half years old. At the time,

Mark was sick with a fever of 104 degrees. After that, Doris and Mark had a rocky relationship. The normally sweet and happy Mark resisted his court ordered weekends with Doris and often called his dad and begged to be taken home before his visits were officially over.

That night Doris offered to take Mark and his twelve-year-old stepsister, Kelly, for the evening. Kelly did not want to go with Doris so she stayed home. Mark did not want to go either, but in his shock he consented. He took only enough clothing for an overnight. But the next day, Doris did not bring Mark home. Nor the next day. Thus began a seven-year struggle to return to the family he loved so much— his stepmom, Sally, stepsister, Kelly, and a stepbrother, Steve.

More Losses

Early Monday morning, Doris went to the Social Security office with Mark to state she was the Mrs. Hanson whose husband had just been killed. She reported that she needed to make arrangements to get his Social Security benefits for Mark and herself. What a surprise was in store for Sally when she reported the death of her husband later in the day and found that the Social Security benefits had already been applied for and all the paperwork had been completed for the former Mrs. Hanson.

Tuesday morning Doris enrolled Mark in a new school and acted as though nothing had happened. Doris did not allow Mark to see or talk to Sally or Kelly. Just prior to the funeral, a Child Development Specialist at Mark's new school contacted me. "Would you please talk to Mark's mother about whether he should attend his father's funeral?" asked the specialist. "And by the way, being that young, Mark shouldn't view his father's body, should he?" I visited Doris' home that same afternoon where I met Mark and his mother. I was unaware of their story prior to this visit. Although he had never seen me before, Mark was delighted to have me there and he clung to me.

Mark was a well-mannered youngster who was obviously hurting inside. As I sat talking to him, he parroted words he had heard said to him, but did not know their meaning. I asked Mark if he had been able to cry. I told him, "Crying isn't weak or for sissies. It takes a real man to cry." "I know," he responded. "Crying releases your emotions." Then I asked, "What kind of emotions are you having, Mark? Can you tell me?" He looked up at me with total innocence and asked, "What are emotions?" We talked for quite a while. As I was about to leave, he snuggled up to me and said, "Don't go. Please, stay a little longer!"

Mark had not been allowed to see or talk to his other family. Mark's pediatrician, the funeral director, and I all agreed that it would be in Mark's best interest if he were to attend the funeral on Wednesday, and if Mark wanted, to let him view the body to know his father's death was a reality. I warned that Mark must be properly prepared in advance of the viewing. Mark did attend the funeral with his mother, Doris.

Grief Surrounded by Family Problems

After the funeral, I saw Mark several times. This was the first grief work I had done with a child alone rather than with an entire family. It did not take long to sense that something more was going on in this child's life than the background that had been shared. Mark clung to me more each time I visited. Often, he looked out to the kitchen to see if Doris was listening to our conversations, then begged, "Can't you stay a little longer?"

Soon I began to notice cuts and scrapes surrounded by large areas of dark deep bruising on his face, arms, and legs. I asked, "Mark, where did you get those awful bruises?" He replied, "Got 'em roller skating. I fall down a lot." I knew that no one got those kinds of injuries by just falling while skating. I wanted to say something, but when I noticed the look of terror in Mark's eyes, I said nothing more. He breathed a sigh of relief. In those days, signs of physical abuse did not have to be reported. In fact, at that time one could be sued for mentioning a possible abusive situation.

From the first visit, thoughts had been spinning in my mind that there was something amiss concerning the relationship between Mark and Doris. I was visiting with Mark once or twice a week at his request, and the request of his school counselor. Whenever Doris came into the room, Mark would become smart mouthed and exhibit obnoxious behavior. He was reticent to talk to me or even answer my questions in front of Doris. It was always difficult for Mark to let me leave.

At the same time, his step family was grieving not only the loss of a husband and stepfather, but also the loss of Mark. Neighbors stopped by to bring flowers, food, and sympathy. One older neighbor, who the children adored, brought a potted geranium for each of the children. She sat and shared memories of her father's death when she was a child. It was so important for Mark to be a part of his grieving family at this time—and he missed it all.

The school counselor called me a few weeks after the funeral. She told me that Mark was doing well scholastically, but was lonely and had no friends. "He is an emotionally upset little boy," she explained, sounding worried. The principal spoke to an older cousin of Mark's who attended the same school. He asked him, "Will you please look out for Mark and try to keep him company?"

Within a month, there was another call from the school counselor. She told me that Mark's stepmother, Sally, desperately wanted to speak with me. Sally asked if I would meet with her and Mark's paternal grandparents. When we met, they told me about Mark's reluctance to see his biological mother even on his court-ordered weekends before Ben's death. Sally also told me that soon after Mark left, his new puppy disappeared and had never been found. In addition, she mentioned that Mark had been taking piano lessons that he enjoyed immensely. Mark told his family how aware he was, even at this young age, that playing the piano was calming for him. Sally and the grandparents talked about what they saw as abuse and general neglect of Mark. This did not surprise me.

Before this family group left, Sally gave me a Manila envelope filled with letters and pictures that Mark's classmates at his old school had written and drawn for him when they heard of his father's death. Sally asked if I would give them to Mark when I saw him. The next time I saw Mark, I attempted to give him the envelope of "treasures." He begged me to keep them for him and he did not even open the envelope to look inside.

I grieved for Mark and all that he had lost. Most children losing a parent find the death almost more than they can handle, but Mark lost his father, his family, his grandparents, his home, his caring neighbors, his school, his friends, his piano, and his new puppy. I felt that his rights as a child had been violated, and I struggled to figure out if there was anything I could do to help him.

Custody Battle

Before the end of the school year, Doris moved them again to a new neighborhood and a new school district. I was not notified as to where they had moved and Mark was not allowed to call me. As Mark's sad story unfolded, I continually asked myself, *How many losses could one small person handle?*

Mark somehow found a way to call his paternal grandparents and he told them his new address and phone number. He begged them to please come to get him. He thought, and rightly so, that the grandparents might have a better chance than his stepmom of talking to Doris, and perhaps even getting her to let them see him. Doris did agree to let the grandparents take him for an afternoon, but only after a solemn promise to bring him back before bedtime. For the first time since the funeral, Mark was able to see, hug, and cry with his family. He was so happy to see everyone. It was a sad departure when he had to return to Doris. He did not know when he might see his other family again, nor did they.

The grandparents and Sally decided to fight for Mark's custody. In the end, the judge determined that Mark should stay with his biological mother, Doris. After talking to Sally's attorney, I shook my head in disbelief, tears streaming down my cheeks. I had been so involved with this little guy that it saddened me to see what was happening and know in my heart how damaging it would be to Mark. It was the first of several times in the 1980s I was to hear a judge pronounce in custody decisions that "blood is thicker than water."

Occasionally, I kept in touch by phone with Sally, but did not see Mark again for quite some time. One day my husband and I were having Sunday dinner after church at our favorite restaurant when Mark, his step family, and his grandparents came in for dinner. When Mark spotted me, he came dashing to our booth, slid in beside me and gave me a great big hug. I asked how he was doing. "Are you happy?" I asked. Big tears coursed their way down his cheeks, but he confused me by replying, "I'm okay." Sally had the chance to see Mark when Doris allowed him to visit his grandparents for the weekend. Occasionally, Mark's grandparents let him stay with Sally and her family during their allowed weekend.

A Surprise Visit

After that, my path did not cross with Mark's for several years. By then, I had started The Dougy Center and I had given up doing the one-on-one grief work that I had done for many years. I did see Sally and we visited when she came to The Dougy Center. She worked as a volunteer receptionist for at least two years.

One day, about five years after I had last seen Mark, he reappeared. I was sitting at my desk in my office at The Dougy Center when, to my utter shock, in walked Mark. He sat down in the rocking chair and we visited. I offered to give Mark the envelope of letters and drawings sent to him by his second grade class when his father died. He shook his head and again told me it still was not the time.

Mark also told me he was trying to get emancipated so he could get away from Doris. He was not having much luck. The age for emancipation in Oregon was sixteen, and he was not quite fifteen. He told me that things had been hard with Doris, but he did not elaborate. It was obvious Mark was distressed and angry. I told him about the Volcano Room in the Center's basement with the punching bag and padded walls and floor. He asked if he could go down there and I readily agreed.

I could hear him hitting the punching bag and it felt as if every expression of Mark's anger swayed the house from the basement to my upstairs office. When Mark finished, I wasn't prepared for what I saw when he returned to my office. His knuckles and the backs of his fingers were bleeding. He was soaked with perspiration, and his face was stained with streams of tears. It was then that the program director and I knew we had to get him some help. We called a fantastic counselor we knew who agreed to meet Mark at the Center the next day at a certain time. The counselor showed up as he promised, but Mark did not come.

Sally and I continued to keep in touch even after she no longer volunteered at The Dougy Center, but it wasn't until I asked to meet with them to request a signed release for their story for this book that I saw Mark again. By this time, Mark was in his late teens. We were visiting in my living room when I remembered the envelope of letters. I asked Mark, "Is *now* a good time for you to have your letters?" He nodded yes. I gave him the packet and he hesitantly opened the envelope, pulled out the letters and pictures, and began reading them. Within minutes he had his head in Sally's lap, sobbing for all he had missed, for all he had lost. Sally sobbed with him.

That day I learned that Mark had run away twice while living with Doris and had been put in detention at the Juvenile Delinquent Home when he was about fourteen. He was released and stayed with his stepsister one time and with Sally another. I also learned about Mark's biological mother's drug addiction. Mark finally was allowed to leave Doris' home and live with his grandparents.

Working with Mark was an eye opener for me. I was attempting to help a grieving child after the death of his father. I was totally naïve about the abusive things that could possibly happen between a biological parent and her child, thinking that Doris would do everything possible to help Mark through his grief and not make it worse. It was difficult for me to realize a parent could be so harsh, abusive, and dishonest with her own child. But perhaps this is what drug addiction does to a person. Mark's experience reaffirmed how important it is for children to share their grief with other children, because they—and only they—speak and understand the same language.

CHAPTER EIGHT

The Workshop:
Children Sharing Their Grief

An experience that had the greatest impact on my journey toward clarifying my vision to create a place for grieving children happened at a southeast Portland public grade school in 1980. Teachers at the Whitman School were ahead of the time, seeking resources to help their students struggling with the death of three students' mother. This situation provided the impetus for the school's search.

A teacher at the grade school called me. "Three of our students have had their world totally shattered because of the unexpected death of their mother," the teacher explained. "The parents are divorced and the father has not been in the picture for years. What we are observing is not grief, not even sadness, but the worst anger you can imagine." The oldest boy in this family, Scott, who was thirteen, had kicked down part of a fence, even with the posts sunk in concrete. "It is frightening for all the children in the school," the teacher continued. "Many children are asking their parents what would happen to them if they, the parents, died." After further explanation, the teacher asked if I would come to talk to the school staff.

I arranged a time to meet with the teachers, school counselor, principal and secretaries. When I arrived, the tension in the room was electric. I was told the ten-year-old twins, Randy and Trina, and their older brother, Scott, had friends throughout the school.

Fragments of the story came slowly at first, then several people began talking at once. Many of the school staff were in tears. "Mom and Dad." "Bitter divorce." "Not long ago." "Kids were out of school with flu, passing it back and forth." The story continued, and I began to understand the children's anger. "And just as the kids were feeling better, their mom got it. She couldn't keep anything down and was dehydrated. Her sister came and drove her to the hospital to get an IV…."

The maternal grandparents came to stay with the children when the doctors perceived a much greater problem than dehydration with the children's mother. The doctors detected a heart defect requiring immediate repair. Because their mom was so ill with flu symptoms and dehydration, her condition was poor and doctors questioned if she could survive the surgical procedure needed to, hopefully, save her life.

After the surgery, their mom was put in the Intensive Care Unit (ICU). The children were not allowed to visit her in the ICU because of hospital rules. At that time, standard hospital rules forbade children to visit, especially in the strictly controlled setting of the ICU. Their mother was too weak to recover. She died without ever seeing her children again. The children were confused and could not believe their mother was dead. They said, "We walked mom to the car. She had the flu. We were sick, too, but we got better." The children were in disbelief. They wanted to know: "What happened? *Who* did *what* to make our mom die?"

At their mother's wake, the children believed that the body they viewed couldn't possibly be her. It did not look anything like their mother. They asked family members, "Why are people telling us things that are not true?" These three children were trying to make sense out of something that seemed totally senseless to them.

After the funeral, their dad sent the grandparents home and he moved back into the children's home with his new girlfriend. Because of the bitter divorce, the children had been angry with their dad. Now, all three children were very unhappy with their dad back in the home, and they were grieving their mother's death.

By the end of my meeting with the school staff they had woven together the whole story. They asked if I would do a small workshop with these children and any others who had experienced a loved one's death or had someone ill who might be expected to die soon. I had done lectures for college and high school classes, and I had worked with dying patients and their families, primarily on a one-to-one basis. This would be a new experience for me, working with a group of children. I agreed to facilitate a workshop for interested children.

My First Children's Workshop

A workshop on death and grieving was a unique experience for Whitman School. The staff and teachers did not want to take chances with this thing called *death*. After meeting with the staff, another meeting was scheduled with the PTA. Repeatedly, parents asked me, "What will you say to the students? What will you *do* with them?"

Still another meeting was necessary—a meeting with parents who wanted to look me over to see what resource materials I would possibly be sharing with their children. They needed to see if they approved of these materials, and of me. The parents would have the final word. In addition, the children who wanted to attend this workshop had to sign permission slips that were countersigned, or not, by their parents. The school was very careful to cover all the concerns.

The day the workshop began it was questionable who was more nervous—the ten children attending the workshop or me. We sat on the floor in a circle in the grade school resource center. I disguised my terror far better than the children, who giggled, squirmed, burped, and bopped each other playfully, yet nervously. Scott, whose mother had died, chose not to attend the workshop; however, his twin siblings both came.

Not wanting to start something too advanced for this group of children, and feeling it would be better to have something a bit too young for them rather than too old, I read them Margaret Wise Brown's *The Dead Bird*. It was a poor choice. Most of them were ten years old and they knew more about this death subject than I could have ever imagined. They did not know how much they knew, but they had experienced it in their lives and, without explanation, had come to their own conclusions. However, these children did not know how to communicate this knowledge or their feelings.

At my request, the small child-size tables had been stocked with paper, crayons, watercolors, and colored pencils for drawing. It was a relief to all of us when I suggested the children get some paper and draw a picture of what ever came to their minds when they heard the word *death*.

A hush came over the room as most of the children became deeply engrossed in their drawings. One girl, Nell, apparently distressed, sat alone at the end of a low table. She was looking at her blank piece of paper, no crayons or pencils nearby. I walked over and sat on the edge of the table next to her, and asked, "Are you stuck?" She nodded, "Yes."

Nell's drawing shows where her puppy was buried in a small black box in the bottom right-hand corner. The tree near the burial spot is dying, its branches bare.

The "apple tree," which can be interpreted as representing the artist, is the center of the drawing. The tree is filled with bright red apples and a ball of healthy green leaves, however, the tree sits on top of the ground with no root system to hold it there. Nell

said the sun with the smiling eye and mouth is happy because "it loved the puppy." Nell's drawing shows the need she had to express her loss.

Then I asked, "Have you ever had a person or pet you loved very much die?"

Suddenly her face lit up and she replied, "Yes, my new puppy."

"How did that feel for you?"

"It made me sad. Really sad."

"Do you think you can draw how you felt or perhaps something that happened after your puppy died?"

"Yes, I think I can now."

I watched with interest as Nell carefully chose her colors. A full sheet of paper lay on the table and with a black crayon she drew and colored in a small rectangle on the very bottom right hand corner. It was indeed *very black*. She looked up at me and smiled. I nodded and whispered quietly, "Good!" Immediately, she took other colors and began to work with excitement on a tree that was filled with leaves and fruit. From the size of the fruit I guessed they were red apples. To the right of this healthy and productive tree, and a short distance away from the black rectangle, was another tree. This tree was bare in contrast to the healthy tree filled with fruit. If there were any leaves, they were falling off the bottom branches. In the upper right hand corner Nell painted a quarter of the sun. Her sun had an eye, a smiling mouth, and eight lines drawn as rays. Nell was the only child who wanted to keep her drawing and take it home.

As I walked around the room to see how other children were doing with their drawings, it was interesting to note that most of them were totally engrossed in working alone on their particular works of art. One boy, Bobby, a bit younger than the rest, was not pleased with his drawing painted in watercolors. The twins and a friend sat at one table together, drawing. All three had a common theme, a bridge that one crosses over when one dies. "On the other side is a beautiful land where there are rainbows, trees, sunshine, butterflies, flowers, beautiful music and you get to see people you loved who have died," explained one of the twins. "There is only one bad thing. You can't *ever* come back across that bridge."

When the children finished drawing their pictures we all went back to sitting in our circle on the floor. There was no more goofing-off. In fact, there was a new seriousness and each of the children appeared eager to share the story told by his or her picture.

One girl, Peggy, had nothing but words on her paper. (See page 84.) In the center of the page a huge "M" colored pink and purple, a large red "a" and another large "d" colored orange. Her picture's title was "My feelings about death." Around the word "Mad" were other words expressing her feelings about death—"sickning," [sic] "Cranky," "sad," "stuned,"[sic] "unloved," "unhappy," "abandoned," "disgusted," "Frightened," "misplaced in time," "Miss-Placed," and "Miss-Understood." Peggy's father had died of cancer and the entire family blamed the doctor and the hospital. The emotion she exhibited most—and no doubt the emotion most felt by her family—anger, is the core of her picture.

I had learned in workshops on "Spontaneous Drawing" that words in a drawing are a possible indication that the individual fears not being understood. Peggy clearly did not want to be misunderstood, so she used lots of words, which are far clearer to the logical mind. A few weeks after this workshop, I had the opportunity to show Peggy's drawing to a psychologist, Gregg Furth, Ph.D., who taught Spontaneous Drawing Workshops. When Gregg looked at Peggy's drawing, he commented, "It takes no graduate degree to comprehend Peggy's message and with a curious, open-ended question, further discourse will open Peggy to share her innermost feelings and attempts to put meaning and purpose to all she has lost and suffered. Her fright, anger, abandonment, and disgust relating to her traumatic situation is the core of her picture."

The twins with their bridge pictures were next in the circle. The bridge explanation is what the twins had been told by the grandparents in hopes this would help the children deal more easily with the death of their mother. Randy's tree looked like a drum major in a band, appearing to have an eye, a nose and a mouth. (See page 85.) The bridge, colored purple, look like an accordion. It was very small and short, not even reaching over the water, which lay below. When I first looked at Randy's picture, I thought, *Could it be this little boy is telling us he cannot bridge the great loss of his mother?* The tiny, yellow-rayed sun in the upper right corner with six outstretched rays seemed to beg the question that life-giving rays are encumbered and limited. The jagged edges of the tree trunk could indicate anger and aggression.

The other twin, Trina, drew a picture of a yellow, stone-arched bridge that extends across the water to land. (See page 86.) When I looked at it, I wondered, *Could this indicate that she is handling her mother's death with more comprehension than her brother is doing?* The empty tree trunk sketched in brown had a lush, healthy green ball of leaves atop the trunk. Green grass and the three colorful tulips were encouraging.

A taller tree with no anthropomorphic indications being touched by the sun's rays could explain that Trina was carrying her mother's death in a more transitional way. However, there was one huge cloud over the bridge. According to Gregg Furth, clouds indicate anxiety over what lies below and this bridge theory of the mother's death did not appear to be satisfying or healing for Trina. Trina's anxiety needed attention, but because of the growth and size of the tree, there seemed a possibility for that growth.

The third bridge picture was drawn by Trina's best friend, Tammy. She held up her picture and began to tell the same story about "when you die you cross the bridge into the beautiful land…." That is where the similarity ended. I wasn't prepared for the story that followed my next question. That story still sends chills through my entire being. "Tammy, why is your bridge so angry?" I asked. Her bridge looked like a mouth with bared teeth, a baby's first weapon. (See page 87.)

She replied angrily, "My bridge isn't angry! Those are the supports that hold the bridge up!" She knew, without my mentioning the brown vertical lines, exactly to what I was referring. My next question came without forethought.

"Tammy, why are *you* so angry?"

There was this ominous silence. It seemed like forever, but then a minute and a half can be forever sometimes. Not a child in the circle moved or said a word. Finally, after gasping for a big breath, her wee soft voice broke through the quiet. "When I was two years old, my daddy died. My mom told me he had gone on a long trip and it would be a long, long time before I would see him again." Then she stopped.

Everyone in the circle sensed she was going to go on. I do not think any of us even breathed while we waited for her to continue. "When I was five years old, I wondered what a two-year-old little girl could have done that was so bad her daddy didn't ever want to see her again."

My heart sank. Everyone waited for someone to make it better. Finally, I asked, "When did your mom tell you your daddy had died? Or has she?" Tammy screamed out so loud that people two blocks away could have heard her with all their doors and windows closed. Then she answered, "Just two years ago. I was eight years old!" Her story was finished. She had no desire to say anything else.

It took a while for all of us to catch our breath before we were able to continue going around the circle looking at the other pictures. *Such openness and honesty!* I thought. There was no way that I, as a neophyte to this kind of children's group, could have prepared for such an impact, for such learning, from these exceptional young teachers.

Bobby was the next child to share his picture. He painted his picture in watercolors, but he was not pleased with his project. (See page 88.) Bobby had painted the word DEATH in capital letters with blue watercolor paint across the entire width of his paper and underlined it with an inch wide band of red. It appeared he then painted a tall red gallows-like rectangle. Not liking the results, Bobby had dipped his brush into the black paint and smeared the paint back and forth across his entire picture. To emphasize his dislike for the picture, or perhaps how distasteful the thought of death was to him, Bobby folded the picture in half, causing the wet black paint to smear even more.

Bobby had been encouraged to come to this workshop because his grandfather was seriously ill and his death was expected very soon. Bobby's parents had hoped he would talk about his grandfather's illness and make some preparation regarding the upcoming death. But that appeared to be the farthest thing from his mind.

"Bobby," I encouraged, "tell me, have you had someone you love die or be very sick? What would you like to share with us?"

Without a moment's hesitation, Bobby began his story as if he had rehearsed it. He must have relived his story endlessly, but it was my guess he had never uttered it out loud before this day.

> "My best friend was my cat. She had a bunch of babies. I wanted to keep those kittens awful bad, but my dad said we couldn't afford to. He said it was all he could do to feed the family and we would have to take the kittens to the Humane Society. He told me they would find good homes for them and the people who got them would love them and take good care of them." He paused, then continued, "We put them in a basket and took them. The lady at the counter liked them a lot and promised to find good homes for every one of them.
>
> "When we got home, my mom acted kinda' funny. She talked to my dad and they finally told me that while we were gone the mama cat had been run over by a car and killed. She said she was sorry and that we could go back to the Humane Society and get one of the mama cat's kittens. I wanted to go right away, but my dad couldn't 'cause he had to go to work. We didn't get back to get one of the kittens until the weekend. We went in and told them what we wanted. The lady looked funny and motioned to my dad to follow her across the room. She whispered something to him and they both looked at me. My dad told me that no one came to adopt the kittens so they had to put them to sleep! But they didn't put them to sleep! They killed them! And when you kill them they can't wake up again! And that's all I have to say!!"

Bobby's story reminded me of an essential lesson about death and grief. Children can be closer to pets than the people in their lives. (This can be true for adults, too.) Children can share their most intimate secrets with their pets, they can even get angry with them, and yet the pets return time after time offering an abundance of unconditional love. Bobby loved his grandfather dearly, but it was his mama cat and the kittens that he associated with the word death and his picture showed how that loss had affected him.

When it was Nell's turn she decided not to speak in the circle about her drawing. I had talked with Nell while she was drawing it.

(See page 60.) I had asked her questions during the drawing process and she was very eager to tell me about it. After returning to the circle, Nell became shy and withdrawn, unwilling to share her story with the group.

At the table, I had asked Nell about her puppy that died. "Did you have a funeral for your puppy or did you do anything special like putting flowers on the grave, sing a song or say a prayer?" She looked up at me, shaking her head "no." She was deep in thought and the thought was distressing to her. Finally, she quietly shared with me what was bothering her. "My dad didn't let us do anything special. I wanted to, and so did my brothers, but my daddy told us to stay far away from that corner of the yard or we would get punished." My arm crept around her shoulders. All I could say was, "I'm sorry, Nell. I'm sorry."

This became a familiar story as I became more involved with children. Parents protect their children from death by not including them in their own pain and in turn, the children protect the parent(s), hoping no one else will disappear.

The following October I received another call from Whitman School. Trina, one of the twins, wanted me to visit them and the school counselor suggested that she might want to organize this reunion. Only four students from the original group were interested, but the ones who were there wanted to let me know what had happened in their lives since May. They also wanted to say thank you. "You listened to us and that made it better," explained one of the girls. "It made a difference."

I hugged each one of them and shared that they had made a difference in my life, also, and that they had been the best teachers I had ever had. The wisdom and sharing of these children would be a major impetus leading to the formation of The Dougy Center. For many of the children, this sharing would begin their journey toward healing.

Understanding ourselves is very much like
the proverbial iceberg, where only one-third
of it can be seen because the rest is
submerged below the water.

GREGG FURTH

CHAPTER NINE

Spontaneous Drawings

One of the most insightful and inspirational experiences I had in the years preceding the opening of The Dougy Center was my introduction to spontaneous drawing. I first learned about this from Gregg Furth, Ph.D., at Elisabeth Kübler-Ross' one-week workshop in 1974. Gregg had been a student of Susan Bach, Ph.D., who was part of a pioneering development in the use of art with patients in mental hospitals. In 1947 Bach discovered that spontaneous drawings accurately reflected somatic as well as psychological states. For many years Bach had an analytical practice and consulted with Carl Jung, applying her research in drawing analysis to seriously ill children.

Gregg graduated from the C.G. Jung Institute in Zurich, Switzerland and went on to teach workshops on spontaneous drawings, symbols, and the unconscious, particularly in relationship to death and grief. Elisabeth was one of Gregg's greatest supporters and she often included him in her own workshops. After taking Gregg's workshops in the 1970s and 1980s, and seeing how much drawings tell us about others and ourselves, I continued taking as many workshops as possible from Gregg. Before long I began organizing and hosting Gregg's workshops in Portland.

Gregg had earned his Ph.D. in psychology with a concentration in Investigation of Drawings as an aid in counseling. He served on the faculty of California State University and John F. Kennedy University. For years, Gregg conducted hospice training services and gave many workshops on drawing interpretation, especially in the areas of death and dying. At the time of his death in 2006, Gregg had spent more than thirty-five years working with emotionally disturbed and terminally ill children and adults.

Throughout most of Gregg's professional life as a psychologist he explored the realm of the unconscious through interpretation of drawings using symbolic analysis to give further understanding to messages from the unconscious. In 1981, Elisabeth wrote *Living with Death and Dying* (Scribner). Gregg wrote a lengthy chapter in that book, "The Use of Drawings Made at Significant Times in One's Life." Gregg wrote his own book about his findings in 1989, *The Secret World of Drawings: Healing through Art* (Sigo Press). A second edition, *The Secret World of Drawings: A Jungian Approach to Healing Through Art*, (Inner City Books) was co-authored by Gregg Furth and Elisabeth Kübler-Ross in 2002.

I learned that analytic interpretation of spontaneous drawings allows people to see their own weaknesses, fears, and negative traits, as well as their strong accomplishments and untapped potential. Gregg believed that spontaneous drawings give us greater insights into others and ourselves. In his book, Gregg stressed that there are no rules or recipes for interpreting spontaneous drawings, but only guides to understanding unconscious content, which is manifested in drawing.

In Gregg's workshops we learned how to "read" spontaneous drawings as a way of understanding to what extent the psyche may be influencing an individual's life. And in the case of the critically ill, what the "inner voice" might have to say about the somatic process. We used Bach's guidelines to evaluate and interpret drawings, considering many questions and observations. Among them:

- What do you see?
- What is in the drawing and what is missing?
- What is odd?
- What objects or subjects stand out and are these merely outline, underscored or filled-in with color?
- How many colors are used?
- Does the person use lots of colors or focus on one or two colors?
- Count any repeated or recurring objects such as sun rays, apples on a tree, windows in a house. Numbers may possibly suggest a significant or important unit of time.
- Colors may symbolize certain feelings, moods, or relationships. They may suggest balance or imbalance in a person's life.
- Colors do not tell the story of a picture, but merely amplify what the objects and action have to say.

■ Notice the placement of objects and people. Is there movement? If so, what direction?

Gregg's handouts for the workshops always included great quotes about getting to know ourselves, the subconscious, drawings, and our "inner voices." He quoted Aristotle: "The soul never thinks without an image." For one of his favorite quotes by C.G. Jung he drew a row of lighted candles, underlining the thought: "The purpose of human existence is to light a candle in the darkness of mere being." Gregg wrote in our workshop handouts that he hoped his workshops on analyzing spontaneous drawings would "encourage us to continue in the search for discovering our wholeness. When this happens the world will be much brighter because we will have learned how to 'light a candle in the darkness of mere being.'" Gregg's influence on my work with grieving children as well as on my own life was illuminating, and ultimately life changing.

Personal Revelations through Drawings

While attending my first workshop with Elisabeth, I heard about Gregg's presentation, "Introduction to Interpretation of Spontaneous Drawings." It sounded interesting, but I did not get hooked at that particular time, perhaps because I was focused on my new mentor, Elisabeth. Two years later, I attended another one of Elisabeth's one-week workshops in Santa Clara, California. Gregg was at this workshop as well, teaching about spontaneous drawings and interpretation. One day, Gregg gave a pre-spontaneous drawing session with a few of us who wanted more in-depth, hands-on information. He asked us to draw a picture of anything that happened to come to mind, but to really get in touch with our being and draw from that perspective.

I do not know what was going on in my head or anywhere else, but I began drawing. For some reason, I drew puzzle pieces, and strangely enough, all but two of the puzzle pieces would have fit together perfectly. I showed my drawing to Gregg who was sitting beside me. I laughed to myself at the absurdity of the drawing. My paper was filled with puzzle pieces all over the page. The two pieces that did not fit together had no parts that would allow them to fit with each other.

When Gregg looked at this drawing, I told him, "They all fit together; but these two do not." He looked at the drawing, then looked at me, and asked very seriously, "And is that all right? Is it all right that some do not fit together?" I wrinkled my brow, not having any idea what he was trying to point out. Again, Gregg asked, "Is it all right that they don't all fit together?" I answered, "Of course it is." Then he dropped the bomb. He asked, "Is it all right for you not to be perfect about everything?"

In that moment, I understood a significant part of my being! All of my life with my mother, everything had to be perfect. If it was not perfect, then my mother insisted it had to be done over, and over, and over. I wondered, *How did Gregg know this from a drawing of what I considered silly puzzle pieces?* After that experience, I wanted to learn as much as I could about spontaneous drawings and understand what they could show me about myself. I was fascinated by how drawings could pull such incredible truths from one's subconscious.

Not long after that workshop, Gregg came to Portland to teach a spontaneous drawing workshop for a long-time friend of his. I attended this workshop and became even more intrigued by what could be learned from these drawings. Before long, I graduated from "Interpretation of Spontaneous Drawings," which explained the basics, and took more advanced workshops on "House/Tree/Person," "Dreams," "Fairy Tales," and "Senoi Indian Dream Work in a Western Culture." All of these more advanced workshops still encompassed the interpretation of the drawings as the basic groundwork. I continued to learn more about myself, and what had been hiding in my subconscious. It was revealing, and it was interesting, and I believe I did some growing that I would not have done without the insights offered by spontaneous drawings.

Allan's Breakthrough

After Gregg's first trip to Portland to give workshops, he stayed as a guest in our home. I had strongly urged Allan to take one of Gregg's workshops. In fact, I bugged him often because I believed it would help Al deal with his life's traumas, such as his mother's death when he was a child. But Allan always said no, in spite of the fact that he and Gregg had become good friends. Finally, I just stopped asking him to attend one of the workshops. However, a couple years later, Allan surprised me when he said he was finally going to take Gregg's workshop.

Gregg held the workshop at our church and I planned to help during lunchtime, but otherwise I would stay away in order to give Al his space. The workshops were always Monday through Friday and it was a tradition for the group to go out for dinner on Thursday evening. Late afternoon, Thursday, I went to the church to clean up the kitchen as I did each day. When I drove into the parking area, I could see through the window that Allan was at the kitchen sink washing dishes—something he rarely did at home or away.

I walked into the church just as the afternoon session was breaking up. Several people came over and gave me a hug. Every one of them had tears in their eyes. Al's eyes were teary, too. When Gregg appeared he, too, had tears. I asked, "What has been going on?" Because of the confidential setting, Gregg told me I would have to ask Al.

That night when Allan and Gregg returned home after dinner, I was sitting in the living room reading. They sat down and began to talk about the afternoon session. Al had brought his drawings home to share with me. With spontaneous drawing exercises we always drew three pictures: one depicting an activity when we were quite young; a second showing something in our life now; and the third drawing was something spontaneous that just came to mind. Stick figures were not allowed, and that was a huge problem for Al who did not consider himself an artist. Gregg was aware that Al's mother died when Al was young, so he asked Al deeper questions as Al shared his drawings with the group. The questions about the drawings brought to the surface many emotions that Al had suppressed since his mother's death.

One of the things that came out as Allan relived his pain was that he and his sister, Katherine, and their two cousins had been sent to the movies the afternoon his mother died. Later, the cousins' mother picked them up and took them to her home for dinner. At the dinner table that evening, their Aunt Margie casually said, "While you were at the movies this afternoon your mother died and her body was taken to the funeral home." Both Allan and Katherine were stunned and even more upset when they found out they would not return to their home that evening. Allan was so angry he did not go to the funeral and spent the rest of his life feeling guilty because he did not go. Al's father remarried shortly after his mother's death, something not uncommon for a widowed man with children. Al's new stepmother was mean to both the children and to their father, but his dad believed that "once you make your bed, you lie in it." So he stayed with her.

I was amazed and overjoyed that Al had shared these painful memories with a room full of workshop participants who had become extremely close as they shared their drawings and their stories. I had prayed that Allan would some day be able to share some of his deepest grief. I give tremendous credit to Gregg's spontaneous drawing workshop for facilitating Al's grief work.

Allan was a different person after taking "Interpretation of Spontaneous Drawings." It freed him of a heavy emotional load he had carried since he was thirteen. Al was lighter and more able to face situations without them burying him back under the grief he had carried for forty-six years. This workshop had truly transformed his life.

After taking many different workshops from Gregg over a six-year period, I began using spontaneous drawings with the people with whom I was working. Drawing was especially good when I worked with children. While the children thought they were just drawing a picture, in fact they were reaching into their subconscious and drawing things that concerned them.

When I worked with ill or dying children, or children and adults in grief, I frequently had them draw pictures. The drawings on pages 84 through 93 were created by some of the children with whom I worked during their illness or in grief workshops.

The miracle of attending Gregg's "Introduction to Interpretation of Spontaneous Drawings" was not only about learning how to interpret drawings as a tool to use with others, but also the interaction of the workshop attendees as they related to each other's stories. I could see a part of myself reflected in each story.

CHAPTER TEN

Becoming a Monster

Late one evening in October 1981, Patty and Johnny were in their living room having a heated argument over finances. Their three boys had gone to bed and were supposedly sound asleep. As the parents continued arguing, they unexpectedly heard their eldest son, seven-year-old Michael, yell out from the top of the stairs, "Daddy, shut up and stop fighting!" This was unlike Michael, a sweet and sensitive boy. His outburst surprised everyone, even Michael. His parents' arguing had upset him, and he wanted to be sure his mom was okay.

Several days later Johnny took his three boys on their yearly trip to the pumpkin patch to search for just the right pumpkin for their Halloween jack-o'-lanterns. He said nothing about Michael yelling at him, and Michael never apologized.

One evening shortly before Halloween, Patty sent Johnny to the store for some groceries so she could make school lunches for the next day. He took his best buddy, Little John, with him. Little John, who had gotten his nickname because he was shorter than Johnny, was considered a part of the family. Little John and Johnny had been partners in car racing events for several years. For the trip to the store, they drove a heavy-duty speed car that both men had been racing. Johnny planned to put a smaller engine in this car the following day so Patty could use it to run errands and to transport the boys around town. What the men did not know was that Patty had changed a flat tire on the car that day. She had tightened the nuts while the car was still on the jack, but did not realize the nuts needed to be tightened further when the tire was back on the ground.

That night the fellows did not come back with the groceries. It got to be later and later, and Patty worried. She began making calls. A family member worked with the police department so Patty started her search there. Then there were calls to hospitals, all to no avail. She walked the floors most of the night, pursuing every thought that entered her mind. There were no answers for Patty or for their three sons when they awakened the next morning. She made more calls, but still no answers. Patty was beginning to think that she was going crazy

At noon the next day a police officer, accompanied by one of the children's uncles, came to Patty's front door. Immediately, Patty knew that what she had suspected through the long night was true. Johnny was dead, as was Little John. They had been traveling at a high speed and a wheel had come off the car. The car crashed into a telephone pole and both men died instantly. Patty presumed that since they had planned to turn the "roaring tiger" race car into a "purring kitten" for her use, they had taken it out for one last high speed run.

Your Daddy Is Dead, Don't Cry

Michael was steeped in shock and confusion when he heard his dad had died. While the policewoman was talking to Patty, Michael's uncle patted Michael on the head and gave him a set of instructions—the same ones given to a host of other little boys through the years, and still today. The story often told to young boys after the death of a father usually goes like this: "You are now the man of the family. You have to be strong and take care of your mom and your little brothers. And don't cry because that will make them sad and cry, too. You just have to be really strong!" That same story was given to my dad when his father died. My dad was seventeen, not seven.

At seven years old, Michael was now declared "the man of the family" and told he needed to "be strong" and "not cry." What did that mean to this little guy who, a few nights before, had yelled at his dad and told him to shut up? Michael had never told him, "I'm sorry" or "I love you" after the incident. How was Michael going to possibly take care of his mom and little brothers when he couldn't make sense out of what happened? Who was going to take care of Michael? Michael also lost Little John, their closest family friend. These were the two most important men in his life.

After the death of his father and their dear friend, Michael's personality changed from the lovable, caring, sensitive child to one who terrorized other students in the classroom and on the playground. Much of the time he ran away from school and could not be found. He fought with his brothers, five-year-old Tom and two-year-old Danny. They were frightened to be around their big brother. Sometimes Michael ran away from home and went to stay with friends of a family who lived in the neighborhood. The neighbors loved Mike and would let his mom know when he was there.

Michael began to hit, bite, and kick, some times kicking holes through the plasterboard walls in the house. Their home was a constant scene of unrest with Mom in the depths of grief, brothers Tom and Danny grieving, and angry relatives scolding Mike for his acting out. This turmoil went on for months. No one was in a state of mind to see *why* Mike was acting out or be able to understand him or help him. In essence, Patty described Michael as a sweet, loving child who was now acting like a monster.

Finding Help

Michael celebrated his eighth birthday in July 1982, nine months after his father's death. Toward the end of August he had an appointment with Allan, who was his pediatrician. Michael needed a physical exam so he could play school sports during the coming year. When the nurse took Mike out of the room to weigh him, Patty told Allan how Mike had been acting for the past nine months and that the entire family was concerned. Allan asked if anything might have happened at the time Michael started acting so differently. Patty poured out her story, happy to have someone willing to listen. Allan listened carefully. He knew Patty well because he had also been *her* pediatrician when she was a child.

Just four months earlier while taking Gregg's workshop Allan finally came to terms with the death of his own mother forty-six years before. Allan understood the trauma and heartbreak that can go on for decades when such a devastating event is never reconciled at the time. Just like Michael, Allan, too, had chosen not to go to a parent's funeral. Michael was truly in the right place at the right time with the right person. Allan wanted to do anything he could to help Michael. Thus, my husband would become my number one advocate for establishing a support program for children who had experienced the death of a family member. Allan completely understood why I wanted to create a program where children could share their feelings, guilt, and fears with other kids who had also experienced the deaths of loved ones.

After talking with Michael, Allan called me and asked if I would be willing to help Michael and his family. We were about to leave town for ten days so I told Al to send Patty and Mike over to our house. I decided I would give them some books to read until our return. When Michael and his mom arrived a short time later, I had two books selected for them. Michael cradled the books in his arms as if they were the greatest treasures on earth. The books were, *Learning to Say Good-bye* by Eda LeShan, and *How It Feels When A Parent Dies* by Jill Krementz. I invited Patty and Michael to sit down and we chatted for quite a while. I talked to Mike and told him about these books. He thought both of them sounded interesting and promised to read them with his mother to see if they would help.

They both responded positively to having someone listen to them *and* care as they spilled out their feelings. Michael looked like a little boy who had lost the center of his being. Worse yet, he told me he felt totally responsible for the loss that all of his family was feeling. Mike honestly believed that if he had not yelled at his dad, then Johnny would still be alive. While he was sitting there, Mike said, "If I had even told him I loved him! I was sorry for yelling at my dad. Now I never can say it!"

Shortly after our return from vacation, Patty was in Allan's office again with one of the other boys. She returned the Jill Krementz book, saying that it had not spoken to Mike's needs. However, they both liked the other book. "Mike has really found help from *Learning To Say Good-bye*. May we keep it a while longer?" Patty asked.

A few weeks later Patty called to ask if they could they keep the book still longer. She said, "Mike has had a cold and I have kept him home from school. With Tom at school and Danny down for his nap, we sit and read it over and over. When I start to cry, Mike tells me, 'Mom, I'll read while you cry and then when I start crying you can read again.'" Patty added, "When his friends come over, he will read parts of the book that he finds particularly meaningful to his friends. I didn't think they would stay and listen, but they do. I can't believe how reading that book has changed Michael." Then Patty admitted, "It has changed me, too."

Allan took a special interest in Michael, and Patty brought him to visit Allan at his office on several different evenings, once Allan had finished with his patients. They made paper airplanes together and flew them. While making the planes, Allan and Michael talked about how much it hurt to have a parent die when you are just a kid. These conversations helped both of them. Between August and December, Michael's violence abated, but he still could not make sense of what had happened, and he still felt guilty about yelling at his father and never apologizing. Somewhere in the back of his mind, Mike continued to believe that he was the cause of his father's death.

At the end of December, the three brothers became a part of the first support group at The Dougy Center, and Patty became a member of the first "Parents' Support Group." (See Chapter Thirteen.) The facilitators noticed Patty was definitely not grieving in the same ways as the other moms. We were all aware that everyone grieves differently, but this was confusing. In fact, the other moms did not know what to make of her. It was as if Patty was in a totally different dimension. It would be years before we were to understand that Patty was secretly struggling with alcoholism.

Around the time the boys became participants in the first children's support group, Patty was dating Donald, a man her boys really liked. They kept finding reasons for getting Donald and Patty together, even though Donald was quite a bit younger than Patty. About two years after Johnny's death, Patty married Donald. The boys seemed ecstatic with this turn of events and a few months after the marriage, they made their closure with The Dougy Center program. The new man in their life helped to ease this family's pain and helped them to find joy in their life again. But this newfound joy was not to last.

As Patty's drinking escalated, she was caught in one lie after another. After nine years of marriage her new husband left, taking two of the boys with him. Michael stayed to look after his mom, but became very bitter toward her, and toward life in general. By now the boys had finished high school and had gone on to new jobs or to college.

Unresolved Grief Years Later

Several years after Johnny's death, and long after I had seen or heard from any of the family, Patty stopped by my home one day after a session with her psychiatrist. This unannounced visit was completely out of the blue. Patty wanted to show me one of her wedding photos from when she had married Johnny. She stayed for more than an hour, talking. Her conversation was confusing to me, and made little sense. Later, I would learn that Patty also had been using drugs in addition to drinking heavily. For several months after her surprise visit, Patty phoned me occasionally. After a while the phone calls stopped. Then a letter arrived from Patty. In it she had enclosed two writings Michael had done for one of his college classes. In one paper Michael wrote:

> Billions of years ago this world started to form. In the world my favorite feeling is happiness. Happiness is a newborn baby, the sun glowing, a flower blooming. Without happiness the world would be dark and dim. As long as there is happiness, life will live forever. If happiness falls to the face of sadness, life will not live as life.
>
> If I could be anything in the world I would be happiness. Everybody has happiness. They may not think so, but they do deep down inside. Happiness will live forever as long as it is remembered. Happiness is life that flows through a person and is a feeling everyone has. I have it and you have it. I am going to try not to lose it, and I hope you will do the same!

But Mike was not happy, nor did he display happiness. His other piece of writing confirmed his ongoing sadness and depression. This was a three-page story entitled, "Religion's Nuts," in which Michael wrote about some of our "infamous preachers (TV evangelists) who preach fidelity and righteousness every Sunday and get nailed for prostitution, the very thing they claim to be a major sin." In this paper Mike wrote despairingly of Christianity, God, and religion. He wrote, "Religion needs to be more fun like it used to be. The stories of mythology are a lot more fun." He added, "I would like to think that if there was really a God that the world would be far better than it is." When I read Mike's writing I began to understand the reason for all his negative feelings toward anything good.

> Probably the largest reason for why I think like I do is death. I was seven years old when my uncle came to the door to tell my mom, my brothers and me that my father had died. I was never the same after that. I became very cold and withdrawn. I spent three years in shock. For those three years I tried to kill myself many times. My mom brought me out of it basically by telling me that if I died she wouldn't be far behind. When I finally did come around I spent the next three

and a half years in therapy. Most people say that it is wrong to blame God for [my dad's] death. They said God needed him for a bigger purpose. As if my needs weren't big enough! For all those people that have told me that, I tell them not to say that to a seven-year-old kid who was too scared to go to his father's funeral.

Michael had taught me a crucial lesson. Adults tell children many things to try to make death easier for them. They tell boys they are now the man of the family, and tell both girls and boys that God needed the person who has died, or not to cry or show sadness because it will make others too sad, too. These attempts at trying to comfort children actually cause more harm.

Follow-Up Twenty Years Later

Years later after a long search, I got back in touch with these three brothers who were part of the first group of children at The Dougy Center. I was certain if one could be found, he could lead me to the others. I reached Danny first. He remembered me and we had a delightful conversation. He told me he lived with his brother, Tom, and Tom's fiancée and her sister. He gave me phone numbers where I could reach both Tom and Michael. Danny said that he and Tom were into sports and that he enjoyed sharing a home with Tom and his fiancée. They planned to continue living together after Tom married. On the other hand, Danny and Tom felt isolated from their brother, Michael, describing him as a "flake."

Before ending my phone conversation with Danny, I asked him what he remembered about his dad. Danny was three years old when his dad died, but there were a couple things he thought he remembered; or that he had remembered hearing his older brothers saying about their dad. "When we were small we would all wait for our dad to come home from work," Danny recalled. "We would all take turns jumping into his arms when he came in the door. It makes me feel good to remember that even now." Danny also talked about how their dad had made them a big toy box, probably four feet by five feet. They would empty it out and make it a boxing ring. "Dad was the referee, and that was fun. And my brothers liked the Incredible Hulk a lot, but he scared me. Dad comforted me."

My phone call with Tom was also enjoyable. He even invited me to his wedding at the end of the month. Tom said he had always been the "bumps and bruises" kind of kid, the mischievous one. He was aware of his mom's drinking, probably when he was in fourth or fifth grade. "There were empty liquor bottles all over the house. It was pretty bad!" Tom admitted. When asked what he remembers about his dad, Tom said, "I have bits and pieces of things I remember when I try to think about what he was like. I sort of have pictures in my mind, but not much more."

When Michael and I connected on the phone, we made a date for lunch. Mike had just turned twenty-nine, and he shared his life willingly. We had a tremendous rapport and I couldn't help but think it was because he loved his pediatrician, Allan, so much. Mike told me he did not feel particularly close to either one of his brothers, but he was very close to his fiancée and her two children, ages ten and thirteen.

When we met, I could not help but notice that Michael carried a lot of weight, as if he was carrying the heaviness of his depression. The extreme pain showed in his eyes, body language, and the way he spoke. I asked Mike what he remembered about his dad. He smiled as if reliving the things he remembered. "He was my best friend. Even when I was seven we were making plans about buying my first car. We knew what kind of car it was going to be. We did a lot of outdoor things together—hunting, fishing, camping. My dad was special." Then Mike added, smiling, "One Easter Sunday when my mom had us all in our new clothes, I went to work with my dad, as I often did, and we did an oil change. You can't imagine how angry my mom was at both of us!"

After I asked Mike if he remembered yelling at his dad and telling him to shut up when his parents were arguing, he frowned and shook his head, "No." But when I asked if he still thought he was responsible for his dad's death, without hesitation Michael said, "Yes." Then he looked down, quiet, the sadness settling in once again. Our conversation was on hold temporarily. Then Mike looked up, and became more animated as he recalled making paper airplanes with his pediatrician. "Dr. C. kept an airplane in my chart and if it didn't happen to fall out when I was seeing him, I would ask him if he still had it. He always did."

When I asked Mike if he was aware of his mom's drinking, he agreed with Tom's time line. Mike said she hid bottles of vodka in the bathroom and went in there, locked the door, and drank until she could barely get from the bathroom to her bed. In spite of this, Mike stayed the longest time at home with his mom. He tried to see her at least once a month, never forgetting his uncle's directions to "be the man of the family."

Mike volunteered that even after all the years, the pain of losing his dad was overwhelming. I asked him if that might be the reason he had had so many traffic accidents and violations, that perhaps unconsciously he, too, was trying to die. He startled me by answering, "I think so." He was close to tears. So was I.

We lingered over lunch long after our dishes were taken away and the bill paid. He seemed totally comfortable being there with me. We had spent more than two hours together, but he was in no hurry to leave. I told him about The Dougy Center's new group for "Young Adults" age nineteen to thirty. He was interested. I assured him I would get information about the group and let him know later that day. It had been almost twenty-two years since the death of Mike's father. I thought, *Perhaps Mike can find a way to heal his pain, the way Allan did, years after the death of a parent.* Hope springs eternal. Allan taught me that lesson!

After seeing Mike and spending time with him, I was very concerned about the depth of his depression. Before long, I called Mike and asked if we could get together. I had done a great deal of thinking since we had seen each other and I wanted to follow up with him again. He immediately agreed, and a week later he came to my home. We were both hungry so we decided to go out for a bite to eat. Over lunch we talked at great length, and continued the discussion when we returned to my home.

I was honest with Mike, telling him, "When I look at you, I am seeing the seven-year-old Mike—very sad and depressed." When I asked Mike if he thought he was depressed, he was quick to agree that he *was* depressed. I confessed that I was concerned about the depth of depression that I was seeing in him. Mike felt he had a lot to be depressed about without having his driver's license or a job, but that most of his pain was still about the loss of his dad, who was his very best friend. He was not sure that pain would ever lessen. "I have been depressed for so long that it is like being an alcoholic or drug addict," explained Mike. "I don't know what it would be like to not be depressed. I might not like it. I am very comfortable in my depression because I am familiar with it and understand it. I don't know what it would be like any other way." As Mike talked, he described his depression as "familiar," "safe," and "my identity." He told me, "It *is* who I am."

I loaned Michael a new book, *Never The Same: Coming to Terms with the Death of a Parent* by Donna Schuurman, the current executive director of The Dougy Center. It is a self-help book for adults who have had a parent die when they were young, and have never reconciled that loss. Mike promised to read it and let me know what he thought, then placed the book carefully in his backpack. He also said he would try the "Young Adults" group at The Dougy Center when they started up again the following month.

A month or so later, while I was away from home, Mike returned the book putting it in my mailbox. Among other things, he said in a note:

> "I have gone back to The Dougy Center.
> Thanks again, Michael"

An Ongoing Journey

The times I have spent with Mike over the years have taught me that even though participants feel they have healed and are ready to leave their Dougy Center support group, in time they may find that there is still more grief that surfaces. Several participants have made closure with their groups and a year or more later decided to return to address things they didn't realize would still be problematic when they were in their original group. After the death, as time goes by, a piece of music or something a friend may casually say, can bring up feelings that have been hidden and unresolved. The Dougy Center is open-ended and people may make a closure at any time that it feels right, but may return at a later date and work on new feelings.

My own grief following the death of my husband has certainly alerted me to unexpected grief popping up long after I thought I had finished grieving. There are certain days like his birthday, our anniversary, or especially Christmas, which he loved and celebrated each year like a kid, that still pull the rug out from under me. Fourteen years after Allan's death, I can hear a song we both loved and still be reduced to tears within seconds. I have come to accept that the goal is not to get over the death, but rather to embrace the loss and grief as a part of my life, and cherish the precious memories that will always be mine.

Gregg Furth, Ph.D., taught many workshops on spontaneous drawing as a way to get in touch with the unconscious or "inner voice" that can tell us about ourselves. He used the guidelines developed by Susan R. Bach, Ph.D., who discovered that spontaneous drawings accurately reflect somatic as well as psychological states—revealing the condition of one's personality, mind, and body—especially at critical moments in one's life.

Using Bach's guidelines for reading drawings as a way of learning about an individual's life, Gregg taught us how to interpret pictorial language. With Gregg's guidance, many volunteers at The Dougy Center learned to use spontaneous drawings as a way to know themselves better, and as a tool to understand the children through their drawings. The following are examples of spontaneous drawings by children with whom I worked individually as well as in grief workshops. To interpret the following drawings, I combined my knowledge of appropriate color references, quadrants of the paper, and what the different objects might symbolize in combination with what was going on with each of the artists. On a couple of occasions I sent Gregg copies of drawings and asked for his insight.

While the children thought they were just drawing a picture, in fact they were reaching into their subconscious and drawing things that concerned them.

PEGGY'S DRAWING
"MY FEELINGS ABOUT DEATH"

At a school workshop, I asked the children to draw what the word "death" meant to them. Peggy, 10, used words to describe her feelings about the death of her father from cancer. She did not want to take any chances that her drawing might be "miss-understood," so her words spelled out her feelings. Peggy had never talked about those feelings until we talked about her drawing at the workshop.

Later, when I shared this drawing with Gregg Furth, he observed, "Her fright, anger, abandonment, and disgust relating to her traumatic situation are the core of her picture." (See Chapter Eight.) Gregg noted that words in a drawing are a possible indication that the individual fears not being understood.

RANDY'S DRAWING

Randy, 10, drew what he had been told by his grandparents about death: "When you die you go across the bridge to a beautiful land, but you can never come back." Randy, his fraternal twin, Trina, and their thirteen-year-old brother, Scott, were struggling with the sudden death of their mother, all of them in shock and angry. The death of their mother was the impetus for organizing a workshop at their school. (See Chapter Eight.)

Randy's bridge looked like an accordion and sat in the middle of the water. The bridge would not take him safely over the water. Was this young boy telling us he could not bridge the great loss of his mother? Randy's tree looked like a drum major with an eye, nose, and a mouth. Gregg Furth noted that if inanimate objects are human-like, anthropomorphic, this could be a sign of regressive behavior and a cry for help. The small, yellow-rayed sun in the upper right corner with six outstretched rays seemed to indicate that life-giving rays were encumbered and limited.

TRINA'S DRAWING

Trina, the fraternal twin of Randy, drew a yellow, stone-arched bridge that extended across the water to land. When I looked at it, I thought this might indicate she was handling her mother's death with more comprehension than her brother. The empty tree trunk sketched in brown had a lush, healthy green ball of leaves atop the trunk. Green grass and the three colorful tulips were encouraging.

A taller tree with no anthropomorphic indications, touched by the sun's rays, indicated that Trina was carrying her mother's death in a more transitional way. However, there was one huge cloud over the bridge. Gregg Furth observed that clouds indicate anxiety over what lies below. The grandparents' bridge theory did not appear to be satisfying or healing for Trina. This anxiety needed attention, but because of the growth and size of her tree, there seemed a possibility for that growth. Gregg Furth explained that houses and trees often represent the artist.

TAMMY'S DRAWING

Tammy was Trina's best friend at school and she had also heard the explanation about death and crossing a bridge. She told this story when she shared her drawing with the other children at the workshop. Her bridge looked angry, like a mouth filled with bared teeth. Tammy's bridge did not extend over the water to the land on either side. I wondered if she, too, did not find the "bridge story" accurate, acceptable, or believable.

Tammy's blotchy and rough tree trunk (her expression of self) indicated anger and aggression. While talking about her drawing, Trina expressed considerable anger when she shared that she was two years old when her daddy had died. Tammy's mom told her that her father had gone on a long trip and would be gone for a long time. Tammy did not learn that her father had died until she was eight years old. (See Chapter Eight.) Despite the expression of anger, Tammy's bright sun and the pretty blue flower represented signs of hope.

BOBBY'S DRAWING

Bobby, 10, was extremely displeased with his watercolor drawing when trying to express what death meant to him. (See Chapter Eight) He wrote out the word death in capital letters across the entire width of his paper and underlined it with an inch-wide band of red. It looked as if he painted a tall red gallows-like rectangle behind the blue letters. Red can indicate warmth and love, but in Bobby's drawing it expressed anger. The blue letters he started with reflected sadness. There appeared to be two animals atop the black line at the top of his page.

Displeased with his drawing, Bobby dipped his brush into the black paint and made crosshatches across the entire paper. Crosshatching expresses extreme anger and anxiety. To emphasize his dislike for the picture, or perhaps how distasteful the thought of death was for him, Bobby folded the picture in half, causing the wet black paint to smear even more.

Bobby's parents had encouraged him to take the school workshop because his grandfather was seriously ill. Instead, what he shared with the other children was his grief and anger over the death of the family cat who was his best friend, and the subsequent loss of her kittens.

BRICE'S DRAWING, "SHIPWRECK"

In the spring of 1981 I asked a young teenage boy, Brice, to draw me a picture of whatever came to his mind. Brice had been in a wheelchair for a few years due to Spinocerebellar degeneration, and he had overheard the doctor's conversation with his mom stating that Brice would never live beyond 19 years old. (See Chapter Four.)

When Brice drew this picture he called "Shipwreck," originally he only had a boat shipwrecked on a sandbar. His mom told him the drawing looked too grim and she suggested he add water, grass, and colors. Brice did as his mother requested, but still the boat was marooned on a sandbar, probably because it had a hole in its hull and it was not going anywhere. The spar to hold up the sail was not grounded in anything and it seemed unlikely that it would hold up the sails for long. I likened the damaged boat to Brice's body. Before the mom's request for green grass and blue water, the situation looked bleak.

BRICE'S DRAWING,
"THE ERUPTION"

Brice drew this picture less than a year after the 1980 eruption of Mt. St. Helen's in Washington State. I was most struck by his building in the forefront, most likely a barn, that had no light within and no windows on the side. If he had meant it to be a house, there was no chimney, no sign of warmth inside, and no sign of light. The building looked fairly hopeless and dark. I wondered if this was a self-portrait with a life-threatening explosion in the background. Brice also criss-crossed his strokes, indicating anxiety. (See Chapter Four.)

BRICE'S DRAWING,
"GOOFY TREE IN OUR BACKYARD"

Brice sent me a drawing of a tree dated May 29, 1981, inspired by a tree growing in his side yard. His mom sent photos of the actual tree to prove it was real. When I first looked at the drawing, I immediately saw the tree as if it was waving good-bye to the setting sun. My interpretation of this drawing was that Brice was saying on a subconscious level, "I'm not going to live very long. I'm going to die." (See Chapter Four.)

SUZANNE'S DRAWING, "A HOUSE"

Suzanne was eighteen months older than her brother, Brice. She had experienced a lot of grief and hurt in her family as well. (See Chapter Four.) When Brice was drawing pictures as a teenager I also asked Suzanne to draw anything that came to mind that expressed her feelings of what home meant to her. She did not want to draw a picture at first, but then agreed. The door of her house hung loose from the hinge side, the windows appeared to be crying, and there was no chimney for warmth. The path lead up to a side of the house with no entrance, not to the front door

When I looked at Suzanne's drawing I saw expressions of a dreadfully unhappy teenager who did not have warm or happy feelings about her home life. Yet, the full sun shining on her tree, her reflection of self, was bearing fruit. (Despite a difficult and unhappy childhood, Suzanne would grow to be a loving and caring mom.)

BRICE'S DRAWING OF HIS HOME

Brice did not give this drawing a title, unlike his other drawings. I considered this drawing a self-portrait. Rather than his choice of red paint to connote love, I saw his use of red as an expression of anger. Brice painted his house predominantly red and black, an indication of despair. There was no chimney for warmth, no light shining through the dark windows, and the bars on the garage door most likely expressed Brice's immobility, lack of freedom, and anxiety due to his illness. As Brice's illness progressed, several years after this painting was drawn, his mobility decreased. Eventually, it became too uncomfortable to sit in his wheelchair. In the final stage of his illness, Brice needed to be carried whenever he wanted to move from one place to another.

The Dougy Letter

Elisabeth Kübler-Ross wrote a special book for Dougy Turno who had written her a letter asking questions about children and death. This was Doug's favorite page in his book.

When we have done all the work we were sent to earth to do — we are allowed to shed our body — which imprisons our soul like a cocoon encloses the future butterfly —

—— and when the time is right we can let go of it and we will be free of pain, free of fears and worries — free as a very beautiful butterfly, returning home to God which is a place where we are never alone — where we continue to grow and to sing and dance, where we are with those we loved (who shed their cocoons earlier) and where we are surrounded with more Love than you can ever imagine!

International Grief Groups

ANITA PADEN

Children from the Congo tell their stories of loss and grief while sitting in a campfire circle, a natural setting in their culture for sharing times. They also sing, and learn about nutrition, health, religion, and more.

DONNA SCHUURMAN

(above) Teens in the "talking room" at the Rainbow House in Kobe, Japan, are "letting go." The circular room was designed so that everyone could see each other.

(left) The sign outside the Japanese "talking room."

ERIC GRISWOLD

The Mural created at The Dougy Center.

The Dougy Center today includes the main house and the newer yellow house, which is for training sessions and staff offices.

PART TWO

The Dougy Center

CHAPTER ELEVEN

Creating The Dougy Center

By 1982 I was completely immersed in the world of death and dying. Elisabeth Kübler-Ross had been mentoring me since 1974, and I had been working for eight years with dying and grieving families on my own. I was also giving lectures and workshops on death and grief. I taught a course at Warner Pacific College in Portland called "From Life and Living to Death and Dying," and I gave lectures on death and dying for a psychology class at Portland State University, and for student nurses at Portland Adventist Medical Center. Repeatedly, I was asked to give lectures for churches and college classes throughout Oregon. People were interested in finding out more about this scary subject called "death." Elisabeth was right. She would often say, "We need to make friends with it."

I was becoming acutely aware that when a death occurred in a family, most of the time the children were left out of everything that followed. I wanted to find a way to support grieving children and I was ruminating over several ideas.

Sharing My Vision

I decided to attend a national conference of The Compassionate Friends, which was held in Portland, Oregon, to learn more about children's grief process. The mission of The Compassionate Friends was, and continues to be, to assist families toward the positive resolution of grief following the death of a child of any age and to provide information to help others be supportive. For seven months I had been seeing a family whose son died of leukemia when he was eighteen months old. (See Chapter Five.) The family was devastated. After the child's death,

I regularly checked in with his family, which included two older sisters who struggled with raw grief. I wanted to be better prepared to help families such as this one.

At the conference I knew for certain I wanted to attend the session, "The Child and Death," a lecture by Mary Brown, Ph.D. She was a psychologist who researched how a child's death affected the rest of the family. I made my way to the meeting room and had found a seat when a lovely young woman with bright red hair in long soft waves and curls came in and sat beside me. I introduced myself to her. "I am Beverly Chappell. Who are you?" She smiled broadly and answered, "I am Beverly, too. Beverly Fulk." We chatted about what each of us was doing and why we were attending the session. After listening to the lecture, we realized we were both interested in traveling the same path—children and grief. We agreed immediately that we were both

Bev Fulk

Bevs, not Beverlys, and ended up attending most of the same sessions that day. We ate lunch together, exchanged phone numbers, and vowed to get together after the conference.

Soon after, we met again and talked about what we both saw as something desperately needed in our society—a support program for children after the death of a loved one. Bev and I were on the same page from the beginning, so we decided to work toward a shared vision immediately.

Finding Support for Our Vision

Bev Fulk was a single parent of three preteen boys. She worked long hours at office jobs in order to take care of household expenses. In that way, we were different. Bev was the only breadwinner in her household. I was a homemaker, which gave me time to give and attend lectures and workshops as well as visit dying patients who were referred to me. However, whenever Bev and I talked about our shared vision we kept focusing on the serious need that no one else seemed to address at that time—support for grieving children.

The big question we faced: Where does one begin on a mission such as this? We wanted to ask organizations if they could catch the spirit of our vision and help us develop a support program for grieving children. Everywhere we went we got the same responses from the professional community: "We see no need for such a program," "Children do not grieve," or, "They are too young." The ongoing message was, "No, we are not interested."

Bev and I thought if we could approach child specialists they would understand and encourage us. My pediatrician husband opened doors for us. We met with child psychologists, child psychiatrists, counselors, staff on neonatal intensive care units, the Chief of Pediatrics, and the Pediatric Oncologist at the local medical school, now called Oregon Health & Science University (OHSU). They all gave us the same reply, adamant in their responses, "No." The Chief of Pediatrics told me, "I don't want people like you messing with my patients' heads." But with my husband's encouragement, Bev and I forged ahead. Allan knew the realities of children and grief firsthand, not only from his work as a pediatrician, but from his own experiences as a child whose mother died.

Discouraged, but still determined, we turned to someone I knew in hospice. At earlier grief conferences I had met Patricia Spradling, one of the founders of Mount Hood Hospice in Sandy, Oregon. When we approached Pat with our idea she graciously opened her door, and her heart, to us. She agreed fully that children needed to grieve, and thought it was a fantastic idea that we wanted to provide a safe place for them. Pat promised to do everything she could to help us realize this dream.

On our first visit to Pat's office, she discussed many things we had not considered previously, such as acquiring a non-profit, 501c3 tax exempt status, building a board of directors, and developing a financial plan. Bev and I were naïve about such matters. When we left Pat's office she put an arm around each of our shoulders and said, "Bev and Bev, you are fortunate for not knowing what is ahead of you. If you did, I doubt you would be so eager to begin this journey."

Oh, how right she was! Had we been wiser about this journey on which we were about to embark, I doubt we would have gone one step further. The adage, "Ignorance is bliss," described our inspired situation well. Neither of us had ever given a thought to the possibility that it might not work or that we were not the ones to make it work.

The First Board of Directors

On the drive home from visiting Pat, Bev and I brainstormed and plotted our next steps. We asked each other, "How does one begin building a board of directors?" That seemed to be the formidable task at hand. When I reflect on those humble beginnings, and how very little either of us knew about what we were attempting to do, it still makes me shake my head in disbelief.

Allan's long-time office nurse suggested we contact James Lane, a law student at Lewis & Clark Law School, who was her son's good friend. Our son, Steve, had recently graduated from Lewis and Clark Northwestern University School of Law, so I understood a law student's challenges. When I met Jim, we had an immediate rapport. I learned that Jim had been a rancher in Southern Oregon when he decided to pursue his dream of being a lawyer. He was a hard working, no pretense kind of guy. Jim became our first board member and the sole board member with any legal training. At the time, he was a third-year law student at Lewis and Clark. Bev and I asked Jim to take on the job of legally forming The Dougy Center as a non-profit. He also handled organizational minutes and legal requirements.

Nearly twenty-five years after Jim became our first board member, I asked him to share some of his recollections about that time and his efforts to launch The Dougy Center:

> I agreed to meet with Mrs. Chappell and was impressed by her sincerity and dedication to establishing a center for grieving children and their families. After discussing my participation in such a project with my wife, I agreed to become a member of the original board of directors for their dream, not yet called The Dougy Center. I had lost a very young son in a hospital accident ten years earlier and felt a particular affinity to the grieving situation that Bev was trying to address.
>
> I had the honor to serve as The Dougy Center's first president for the first six years of its growth. I videotaped training sessions, helped paint rooms when The Dougy Center moved to the Warner Pacific house, and helped with various fund raisers. I also attended to the

legal needs of the organization and spent hours helping Bev solve the problems and growing pains of the fledgling Dougy Center. To this day, I still want to be involved. Someday I hope to be able to become a facilitator because I think this would be the most rewarding experience of all.

Pat Spradling's advice to immediately form a board was invaluable, especially since Bev Fulk and I had no idea what we were doing. (Fortunately, Pat agreed to be on our first board of directors.) We did know we needed a Certified Public Accountant (CPA). With no finances at all, we needed to persuade a CPA that our work with The Dougy Center was a truly important venture. A dear friend of mine from church, who had known about my dream of a children's grief support program, gave me a suggestion. She had worked for Einar Nordahl, a CPA at the law firm Peak, Marwick, Mitchell. My friend strongly suggested we ask Einar to join The Dougy Center's first board of directors.

Einar agreed to join the board, but years later he admitted that when I asked him to serve as a board member his first reaction was to turn down my invitation. He had just finished serving six years on the board of Marylhurst University and that board had experienced some difficult financial times. Einar was not sure he wanted to get involved with the start of another organization with limited resources. At that time, Einar was not interested in the grieving process; however, he could see that we really needed his help. In addition, his wife strongly encouraged him to join the board, knowing his experience as a CPA would help us tremendously.

While we were pulling together all the pieces to make The Dougy Center a non-profit organization Einar was a task master, and that was what we needed. In those first years, all of us who were attending the board meetings felt Einar's approach went a bit too far. For example, we did not always start each board meeting exactly on time because we were usually waiting for everyone to arrive. When an hour was up, Einar would get up, leave the meeting, and go home. As far as Einar was concerned, he had volunteered his hour as a board member. In spite of being angry at his impatience, it really did get people to the board meetings on time, and the meetings became more efficient, thanks to Einar. In time, we simmered down and did things Einar's style because it worked. He helped us establish what a board meeting was expected to be.

Years later, I asked Einar what he recalled of those early days on the board of directors. Einar told me:

> My experience with grieving was limited. I never knew my grandparents, and until my father died after a long life, there were no deaths in my immediate family. Even though I was involved with The Dougy Center at its inception and understood the need, it didn't really hit home until my wife died many years later. Except for my family, I received little support from others. I don't know if the lack of support was because of who I am or if this is common to most men who have lost a spouse. I now know how important a place like The Dougy Center is for those who need support in their grieving.

One of the first members of the original board was Kim Wilcox. He was the youngest member, and an exceptionally bright young man. I thought he and Einar would make a terrific CPA team. Einar had years of experience, and Kim was aware of the latest accounting information. Kim's family and ours had been friends since the late 1950s, and that friendship has continued over the years. Kim and Einar were a great help as we all learned what it took to build an organization from a living room gathering to a functioning and funded mature nonprofit with its own building. There were many peaks and valleys along the way, and Einar and Kim helped us keep our financial balance. While working on this book, I asked Kim to write his recollections as a founding member of The Dougy Center board.

> In the beginning, it was Bev Chappell talking to my mother in the basement of our home about setting up a nonprofit program for grieving kids. I had just left a large international CPA firm to start my own CPA practice and I was working out of the basement of my parents' home. Bev and Al Chappell were bowling buddies with my parents. My parents taught their kids swimming, and Al had been our family pediatrician. I had played on the tennis team with their son, and during most of high school I had a crush on their daughter. So, our families were connected in many ways.
>
> At the time Bev asked me to join the board of directors I was married, no kids, and really committed to developing a business to sup-

port my family. Spending time helping Bev and Al start a nonprofit for an issue like grief just didn't seem like a good use of my developmental time. So I managed to "hide" during the first couple of meetings that Bev and my mother had, and really tried to avoid helping with the bookkeeping and accounting.

After the second time I ducked out of a meeting, my parents sat me down and suggested strongly that I get involved and help—and they said they would help, too. They offered to do the bookkeeping as long as I did the budgeting, financial statements, tax returns, and attended the meetings. It still didn't sound like fun and the board members sounded really old—I was twenty-seven at the time. And I thought, "The grief issue was something that you recovered from in a week, didn't you?" The board meetings were lengthy, the other people attending were all concerned about this new organization, and all were more knowledgeable than myself. But it was interesting and it was the first time I had been involved in the startup of a nonprofit that seemed to really have a ground swell of need. Even I could see that!

During this initial time my wife found out she was pregnant. This child would be my parents' first grandchild and it was a wonderful time. My wife's mother had moved back to Oregon from California after a rocky divorce and she was going to be here for this wonderful pregnancy. Several months before the due date my mother-in-law fell sick with what she suspected was the flu. She went to the emergency room to find out for certain. Unfortunately, it was not the flu but an inoperable brain cancer.

About three months later my mother-in-law died of a cerebral hemorrhage. Shock was the least of it. My wife was not quite eight months pregnant. She had visualized spending the last part of her pregnancy with her mother. After all, the doctors had given her mom at least six months. Her services were set for three days after her death, and our daughter was born during the service. In my wife's world, grief was something you dealt with and got over, no need for outside help. Our daughter was her only child and the only link with her mother. The impact of my wife's grief response changed all of our worlds forever. I was, from then on, an outsider in her world. We were divorced almost a year later. Needless to say, I saw firsthand why The Dougy Center is magical and why its mission is so very important.

I spent over thirteen years on the board, and I will always be a supporter of The Dougy Center. The most recent bonus of working with The Dougy Center was meeting my present wife at a fund raiser. I met this wonderful lady in the silent auction line—and I fell in love before we finished the line. The Dougy Center truly is a magical place.

Our first board of directors included thirteen people from the community, including Bev and me. We regularly updated the board on what was happening in the organizational process and shared with them how fast the program was growing in those early years,

At least five board members did not stay long, among them a psychiatrist and a counselor. Even though most of them believed children needed a place where they could share their stories and support one another, they decided not to be a part of The Dougy Center's fledgling efforts. Perhaps they saw how daunting the task at hand would be.

My husband was also among the first board members. As a pediatrician, Allan certainly understood the need for such a program. That is why he was so helpful with the organizing from the start; plus, he referred many of his patients with grief issues to The Dougy Center.

Finding Money to Realize Our Vision

Hand-in-hand with establishing a solid board of directors, Bev and I had to turn to the daunting task of finding money to support our vision. As part of our initial fund-raising efforts, we canvassed large philanthropic organizations, but they wanted to see a track record with donations from other organizations before they would support our efforts. Fortunately, board member Jim Lane's mother-in-law belonged to the Portland Woman's Union, a local organization set up to provide financial help for young women. With help from Jim's mother, the Portland Women's Union was able to broaden the scope of their planned giving to provide $2,000 in funding for The Dougy Center.

In 1986, The Dougy Center received its first large grant. The Fred Meyer Foundation (now The Meyer Memorial Trust) gave a three-year grant for $150,000. The first year was an outright grant of $35,000, with a matching $35,000 grant, which we successfully matched. The second year we received a $50,000 matching grant, raising one dollar for every dollar gifted from The Fred Meyer Foundation. The third year we had to raise two dollars for every one dollar of a $30,000 grant. We accomplished this, too. This generous grant gave us the capital to become self-sufficient, and allowed our vision of a children's grief support program to survive and grow.

During those first years, struggling to meet expenses always felt like boulders in our path. Our learning curve was steep, but we made tremendous progress. We had to develop rules for fund-raising activities and set standards for appropriate and inappropriate funding events. We made a few mistakes along the way. For example, at one point The Dougy Center thought it would be a beneficiary of an infant and youth swimming program fund-raiser that ended up not being a good choice. In actuality, they were planning that *we* were to fund *them*, not the other way around. Then there was the time that, as the Center's representative, I accepted the proceeds of "Salty's Wet T-shirt Contest." Our Center's children and their mothers had been invited to this luncheon fund-raiser, but with the wet T-shirt contest featuring women who had been drinking, we quickly realized it was one of our poorer choices. However, our group efforts prevailed and we did meet the requirements of the match grants from The Fred Meyer Foundation. We were on our way.

The founding board members who stayed became vitally interested in the program we were attempting to initiate and they built the framework for the Center to function as a successful nonprofit organization. More energetic and resourceful board members soon joined us. Without those brave souls The Dougy Center never would have survived those early years.

CHAPTER TWELVE

The First Support Groups

Our vision was to create a safe place where grieving children could share their experiences with other children, and receive loving support as they healed. While taking the first steps toward realizing that vision, Bev Fulk and I had both read a book that greatly influenced us: *There is a Rainbow Behind Every Dark Cloud* by Gerald Jampolsky, M.D. Jampolsky is a psychiatrist who founded The Center for Attitudinal Healing in 1975 located in Tiburon, California. The book is a collection of stories and drawings by children facing catastrophic illnesses. Formerly on the staff at University of California Medical Center in San Francisco, Jampolsky wanted to create a safe place where children with cancer could talk. The center's vision was, and continues to be, the belief in ordinary people's extraordinary abilities to help one another. Jampolsky also promoted the idea that each of us has the power to choose our attitude in any given moment, regardless of circumstances.

Another book from the Center for Attitudinal Healing, *Straight from the Siblings: Another Look at the Rainbow*, was published in 1982. This book was written by and for children who had brothers and sisters with a life-threatening illness. It told about the peer support groups sponsored by The Center for Attitudinal Healing where children in similar situations supported one another. We were impressed with what this center was doing on behalf of children and with the success of the children's support groups.

Bev and I decided to learn more about these support groups, so we drove to Tiburon, California, which is about a twelve-hour drive from Portland. We spent a couple of days observing the support groups, asking questions, and getting to know the wonderful people at the center. They supported us in every conceivable way and we learned so much that would help us take the next steps in establishing our support group for grieving children. We saw and experienced the magic of what support groups were doing in Tiburon and knew for certain this is what we needed to do.

Jampolsky was out of town while we were there, but during our visit we were fortunate to meet Tom Pinkson, Ph.D., who would become our lifeline between what their center was doing and what we wanted to do. He told us if we ever needed his help to let him know—and let him know, we did. When we left the center to return to Portland, we were inspired and energized to start our own center for grieving children.

As Bev and I found people who might be interested in what we were planning to do, many people stepped forward to help create what would become The Dougy Center. Early in our gathering process we met a woman, Jenny Stamer, who was so excited about our hopes and dreams that she became a founding board member for a brief time. One day she opened her home for a special meeting for all of those who were interested in a grief support group for children. For a long afternoon we brainstormed as we drank fresh-squeezed orange juice and ate finger sandwiches. About fourteen of us accomplished a mountain of planning, further energizing our vision.

BEV CHAPPELL

Four boys made up the first ongoing children's group at The Dougy Center.

From April to December 1982, Bev and I continued to meet with a variety of interested people and develop our plan. Among them were Shirley Flenner who became a board member, and Coni Lloyd and Lucy Petersen who became facilitators. We also continued to meet with a group of interested individuals whom we had originally met when Tom Pinkson visited us in Portland and taught us how to run a support group similar to the ones they had at The Center for Attitudinal Healing. The input from all of these people was vital as we brainstormed.

The First Children

On December 29, 1982, we held the first children's grief support group in Allan's and my home. There were four children in that first group. Two of the children were Mike and Tom. Their father had died in a car crash with his best friend. (See Chapter Ten.) Their younger brother, Danny, was not yet five, and at first we thought he was not old enough to participate in the children's group. Danny's mom took him shopping with her while his two older brothers, Mike and Tom, attended the first meeting.

An eight-year-old boy whose father had died of a brain tumor also joined the group, as did Nancy, a fourteen-year-old girl whose father had a cardiac arrest and died instantly while he was mowing the lawn. At that initial meeting the children did not interact much, but were all very busy drawing pictures that spoke volumes. When the meeting was over they wanted to know how soon we were going to have another meeting.

After that first meeting, we got a phone call from Mike and Tom's mom, Patty. She told us their little brother, Danny, had cried and felt left out. Danny had told his mom, "My daddy died, too. Why can't I come?" So, we decided to add Danny to the group. The fourteen-year-old girl dropped out right away because she said the other children were "much too young."

The next meeting was almost a month later, and the kids all said it was not often enough. They wanted to meet every week, so we tried it. We soon realized weekly was too often; it interfered with family, school, sports, and church events. Finally, we settled on every other week and that seemed to be perfect.

When we began the program, we decided our policy would be that children could only be a part of a group if accompanied by a parent. If it had been a sibling death, one or both parents were asked to be there with their child or children. If a parent died, the surviving parent accompanied them.

While Bev and I met with the children in our family room, the mothers sat in our living room and stared at their feet. They didn't talk to each other at all, even though they all shared the common denominator of their husbands dying. After only two meetings, we officially began a parent group and Bev Fulk was the facilitator.

For a couple of months we met with the four little boys who we considered the first children's group. Then we added two girls, six and eight, whose father had died of cancer. Up to that point, all the children had experienced the death of a father.

Children as Teachers

From the very first meeting we understood that we had the best teachers in the world to help us learn the fine points of facilitating this new support program. The master educators for us were the children themselves. They were walking through this painful new phase of their lives—the death of a loved one—firsthand. They knew what they were talking about, and what they needed.

We had not thought about how long these meetings should be, and waited to see how it would work out, letting the children and parents decide. It didn't take long for us to realize that the meetings were lasting about one-and-a-half hours. The participants, whether children or parents, were showing us what they needed to do in order to heal.

We opened each support group with a sharing circle, and then let the children do, within limits, what they felt best expressed their feelings. Most of the kids drew pictures, and some sat and talked. One of the little girls just wanted to curl up and snuggle next to a facilitator where it felt safe. So we let her. The room was stocked with drawing paper, colored pencils, and crayons, and there was an assortment of stuffed animals. The kids taught us early along that teddy bears were the animals of their choice—and there were many.

Just about two months after starting the support group, two boys, Bob, thirteen and Pan, eleven, joined the group. Both of these boys had lost their fathers because of heart-related problems. Allan was Bob's pediatrician and he referred the boy to our support group. Pan came with his mother, Izetta Smith, who had first learned about me from Elisabeth Kübler-Ross. Izetta's former husband, a professor, had died of a heart attack. Pan had been living with his father in Olympia, Washington. Izetta had spent years as a professional theatre artist on the East Coast and had recently moved to Oregon. She had just begun exploring a new venture helping traumatized children to heal. Instead, she found herself instantly helping her own traumatized child who was grieving after his father's sudden death.

When Izetta brought Pan to our support group, she immediately saw the need for someone to co-facilitate the parents' group with Bev Fulk; the mothers were not doing much interacting. Izetta began by sharing the challenges she faced as a mother of a newly grieving child. This helped the other moms start sharing more. Thus, the second support group began to gel.

Little Danny fit in well with the children's group. The dynamics among the three brothers taught us a lot about how differently each sibling grieved, and how different the memories were for each child. When Mike started to share some things about their dad one evening, Tom spoke up angrily, and said, "Mike, that isn't the way it was. It didn't happen like that!" And Mike yelled back, "Yes, that is the way it happened." Danny came close to crying at these times because he didn't know who to believe. As young as he was when it happened, Danny had limited information and memories. We learned from these three brothers that each person has his or her own, individual relationship with the one who died, and sees things from his or her own unique viewpoint.

Drawing pictures was a major activity during the children's meetings. This always seemed to bring things to the surface for the kids. Feelings that had been deeply hidden—even from the children themselves—seemed to surface when they were drawing. Most of the children's facilitators had taken the "Interpretation of Spontaneous Drawings" workshop taught by Gregg Furth. We would have enjoyed looking at those drawings in more depth, but the children wanted to put their pictures in the fireplace. They would have one of us set their drawing on fire with a match, and then they told the group that the smoke would take their drawings and notes of love up to the spirits of their dads. That is when our grief as facilitators began to surface.

Before the drawings went up into flames in the fireplace, we would ask if the children wanted to talk about the pictures they had drawn. All the children had felt quite safe drawing, but they were hesitant to talk about their pictures. When one child eventually felt safe enough to talk, it helped the others open up. Before long, the children could hardly wait to talk about what they had drawn.

We facilitators became closely bonded in those first few months. After the children and their parents left for home, we would sit and review the evening. We would ask each other, "Well, what happened? The children and moms seem to love being here, but has being here provided them with any healing? And, what about us? Have we learned anything from doing this?"

Before long, we started having pre-meetings to discuss who might be coming and with what issues. We also talked about issues each of us brought to the meeting so we could get our own concerns and feelings out of the way before we dealt with the problems of the participants. In our post-meetings, we explored our own hidden griefs as facilitators that were opened up during the group gathering. The facilitators became a close-knit group. We learned how to be a great support to one another as well as to the children and parents.

Listening with Love

Beginning with the first support group, we knew that our technique for support would be active listening, or what we called listening with love. What we offered was different from therapy or counseling, which involve active intervention techniques. While these are powerful and beneficial tools and can provide marked changes in clients, they also carry the responsibility for the changes they bring about. The support we offered as facilitators was not intervention, but rather active listening with love. We also trusted that grieving children helping one another was powerful and safe.

When we listened to the children or the adults, we found that was the best support we could offer them. We listened carefully to their experiences, fears, thoughts, and memories. We acknowledged their difficulties and we reinforced their successes, all the time trusting each one's process for grieving and healing. We did not offer advice, solutions, suggestions, or criticisms. Our support was the assurance that the person speaking, regardless of age, would come up with his or her own best answers. We quickly learned that whether a person was three years old or ninety years old, he or she could move toward healing when others listened with love. To this day, The Dougy Center bases its support on listening with love.

Before long, parents began to understand the tremendous value in listening to their children's grief with love. They also learned to be honest with their children about their own grief. It is one thing to tell a child, "It's okay to cry," but it is a powerful truth for a child to witness his or her parent(s) crying as they express grief. Often, parents hide their tears from their children, thinking to shield them from pain. But children can sense unspoken feelings in their parents. Honesty is the best policy, even when answering children's questions about death and grief. If it is safe, a child will ask questions, and set the pace and the depth of the conversation. Parents just have to listen carefully.

The story of a little boy, Ian, and his father, Michael, illustrates so well the concept of listening with love and responding honestly to a child's questions about illness and death. Ian's mother had died from cancer when he was only three years old. Following his mother's death, Ian became introverted and baby-like. "He wasn't a normal, gregarious

The children voted Teddy Bears as their favorite stuffed animal, and they were everywhere.

BEVERLY CHAPPELL

three-year-old," Michael explained. "Ian didn't run and jump. He would lie on the floor and tell me, 'Please pick me up. I'm stuck.' Now I understand that he wasn't stuck on the floor, he was stuck in his grief." Soon after that Michael found out about The Dougy Center, which became a tremendous help for him and his son.

In 1988, Izetta Smith wrote an article about Ian's process for understanding and accepting his mother's death. This story exemplifies the healing that can take place when a child feels listened to, and safe enough to ask questions—many questions. Izetta's excerpt was published in *Bearhouse Chronicles*, the original Dougy Center newsletter.

There was a little three-year-old boy who came to The Dougy Center for a year. He was in the habit of asking his father to tell him the story about his mommy's death every night before he went to sleep. Over the months the story developed and became more and more complete, until Dad was telling him what cancer cells were and how they grew. Little Ian would say, "Why do they grow?" And Dad would say, "I don't know." Then Ian would say, "Where do they go?" Dad would explain the organs.

The next night Ian would say, "Tell me about the organs." Dad would tell him about the organs again.

Ian would ask, "Where is Mommy now?" Dad would explain, in the ways he believed, about her body and about her spirit.

Ian would continue to ask, "Where is her body now?" Dad would repeat his story.

Soon Dad began to talk about cremation. Eventually, Dad took Ian to the funeral home and the funeral director drew Ian a picture of a crematorium and brought Ian the ashes of a dead body. Ian touched the ashes. He asked about the crematorium night after night. Then Ian asked, "Where are Mommy's ashes?" Dad told him.

Ian and Dad went to see Mommy's ashes and he sifted his fingers through them. He asked about Mommy's ashes for weeks and weeks.

During a six-month process, Ian would ask for the story about Mommy. At the end of this time, he would put his thumb and his forefinger about an inch away from one another and say to his dad, "I only have this much more sadness in my heart."

Ian grew from a very sallow, withdrawn child to a robust four-year-old, socially comfortable and assertive. We understood his exploration of the abstract concepts and words as being his way of integrating the "goneness" of his mother. His curiosity, his genuine exploration was accepted and supported by the adults around him. Even if at times it was very hard for Dad to continue to tell this story, still there was a respect for Ian's exploration that helped Dad overcome his own fragility.

The health and resilience of this young four-year-old is a testimony to a child's repetitive, cognitive exploration as part of the foundation of a young child's grieving process.

Bev Chappell with Silas,
the youngest participant at two-
and-a-half years old. This photo
was used on the cover
of a publication,
This Week Magazine.

CHAPTER THIRTEEN

The Early Years of
The Dougy Center

After about a year, the support group outgrew our home. The family room in our basement had served us well, but now there were eight children and four facilitators that more than filled that small room. Upstairs there were five mothers and three facilitators in the living room. We needed to find a larger space, so we began the search at once.

A church allowed us to use their formal boardroom—complete with large tables and tall, stiff chairs. It was nice of the church to help us, but the environment was much too formal for the children. When they sat in the office chairs, their feet dangled far from the floor. It was if they just could not get grounded in this boardroom environment. We tried meeting in several other places, and finally found the perfect house. It suited our needs; we could use it free of charge; and it was in Southeast Portland, not too far from my home. For the first time we experienced enough space to do the things we needed to do with children from ages five to early teens. The children and facilitators met on the third floor and the mothers met on the first floor.

We had been in this house for about four months when we ran into some trouble. The owners of the house were very disheartened one evening when we became quite noisy. We had brought balloons for the kids to blow up and to draw faces on the balloons that expressed their feelings. One balloon accidentally popped and suddenly, chaos broke loose. The kids began blowing up balloons and popping them any way they could, whether it was stomping on them, putting them under the leg of a bench, or in the case of one five-year-old boy, biting the blown-up balloon with his teeth. He asked me to blow up one balloon after another. I would tie a knot on the end and he would put it up to his mouth and bite it until it exploded in his face. Balloon after balloon, I watched as this precious little face become nothing but a mouth full of bared teeth as he bit and exploded balloons.

The Warner Pacific House

After that evening of balloon popping, the caretakers asked us to leave this wonderful place. It had been a perfect arrangement and we were sad to leave. Once again, we were back to holding the support groups in my home.

The Warner Pacific House

I had stayed in touch with many of the people I had known when I taught at Warner Pacific College. One day I went to the college's office and told Roberta Peterson, an administrative assistant, about our need for space. I asked if we might possibly use their gymnasium one evening every other week. She talked to the right people, pleading our cause, and before long the college offered us the use of an empty house on the periphery of the campus. The only caveat for using the house was that we had to first do much-needed repair work, and then clean it. The house had been used for classes and there were sheetrock walls where walls should not have been, and no walls where walls were needed. The house had been empty for a long time and was filthy. Despite the problems, my response was, "Yes, indeed, we will clean it and fix it and make it usable."

At this transitional time we were in great need of help. Fortunately, The Skyline Council of the Oregon Chapter of the Telephone Pioneers came into our lives with help from Dougy Turno's mother, Carol. She was a Southern Bell Telephone employee in Aiken, South Carolina, and

I had kept in constant touch with Carol ever since she and Doug had been in Portland a year and a half earlier. When I mentioned to Carol we needed help, she put me in touch with the Skyline Council Pioneers. At Carol's insistence, I called the Oregon chapter and asked if they could help us secure an electric typewriter, not expecting anything more.

Bev Chappell with Jean de Lacey Bourke of the Skyline Council Telephone Pioneers

We were trying to get The Dougy Center's new home functioning and we had little to nothing to work with. The request for a typewriter was relayed to Jean de Lacey Bourke, president of the council. Within days Jean called with the good news that she had a used typewriter. She offered to deliver it to The Dougy Center so she could see our new headquarters. Several of the folks on the Skyline Council's board came with Jean. Recalling that visit years later, Jean laughed and told me, "We entered through the back door, which was open, to find you, Bev, on your hands and knees, scrubbing the kitchen floor." Then she asked me, "Do you remember how pleased you were to show off your new quarters, which needed so much work? On our way back to the office Skyline board members started talking about taking on The Dougy Center as a council community service project, and so we did."

Many members of The Skyline Council spent quite a few weekends cleaning, scrubbing, painting, and repairing the new home for The Dougy Center. When the Pioneers and so many others came to our rescue to clean this downtrodden house, we were all delighted. Many people worked hard at many projects, from knocking down walls to plastering to painting. Coni Lloyd, one of the early volunteers, was artistically talented and she painted a mural in the children's meeting room to brighten it. All of us were thrilled with our accomplishments. Recalling those early years at the Warner Pacific house, Jean described in a letter the Pioneers' next step on behalf of The Dougy Center:

> A few months passed and one of the council members suggested that the money we had accumulated from Pioneer sales could be used to supply The Dougy Center with furniture for a Christmas gift. One of our members contacted a furniture store, explaining what we were doing and the store gave us a wonderful offer. We were able to purchase a sofa, two end tables, a couple of easy chairs and two lamps at far less than their regular cost. Bless the furniture store; they even delivered it all to The Dougy Center.

The Pioneers also gave us dishes, cutlery, cups, glasses, a stove, refrigerator, and dishwasher. This house was beginning to look like the safe, warm nest we wanted for the families who would come. It was already feeling like that for those of us who worked there. Without a doubt the Telephone Pioneers were essential to the beginning of The Dougy Center. They assisted at a time when our needs were overwhelming. It felt as if Dougy Turno's spirit infused our new home through his mom's fellow employees in Oregon. On February 29, 1984, this quaint fixer-upper house became The Dougy Center's home for more than four years.

A Cadre of Angels

Another group of special angels who came to the aid of The Dougy Center in those early days was the Loma Linda University Medical Auxiliary/Portland Chapter, headed by Linda Usher and Sandy Bingham. The members were wives of physicians on the staff at Portland Adventist Medical Center. My husband was also on the staff at this hospital.

This medical auxiliary had a tradition of supporting projects around the world. When the members heard about the needs of The Dougy Center, they thought having a local project would be worthwhile. Linda had told the auxiliary, "We need a purpose—a mission." Since Linda's interests revolved around children, she had made a list of possible

In the early days, the Center hosted pot luck meals before meetings.

projects, putting The Dougy Center first on her list. She knew little about our vision other than we needed a place where we could help children deal with death and grief and she respected that I had a strong sense of what grieving children needed. Linda also knew my husband was a pediatrician on the same hospital staff as her husband.

Linda made an appointment to meet me at our small house at Warner Pacific College. During our meeting I had to laugh when she told me most emphatically, "By the way, I don't do death and dying. That said, I *do* do children." Linda was impressed by both our desire to help children and by The Dougy Center's many needs. In turn, all of the auxiliary members willingly said, "We will help. Tell us how we can."

The auxiliary members' introduction to the workings of The Dougy Center was as "house parents" for a brand new group of children. Linda later told me that the experience was profound, one she would never forget. She also admitted that the situation with the participant families was far worse than they had anticipated. In the early days of the program, there were potluck meals before the meetings. The children loved that there were meals because most of their parents were so steeped in grief they no longer cooked at home. Often, families ate at a variety of fast food places, grabbing a bite to eat on their way to the Center. Jenny, one of the early kids whose dad had died, told me, "We love the food we get to eat here. Our car is filled with fast-food wrappers where we used to stop before coming to The Dougy Center. My mom doesn't cook any more."

These auxiliary "moms" and the Pioneers were the best things that could have happened to The Dougy Center. They were determined to help make this program work. And with help and love from these volunteers, the program worked!

Linda Usher and Sandy Bingham joined the board of directors because they saw the value of what we were trying to create at The Dougy Center. Linda served on the board of directors for five years and Sandy served for three. While they were house parents they saw people healing. Our new Center offered grieving children and their families nutritious food, conversations, laughter, and homey comfort. Linda told me, "Breaking bread together is an important concept. We saw it on a grand scale."

The Principles of The Dougy Center

As we worked out the logistics of where to hold our support groups, train new facilitators, and reach out to the community, we also clarified the principles that would guide us. From the beginning, we knew the mission of The Dougy Center was to provide loving support in a safe place where grieving children could share their experiences as they moved through the healing process. We intended for The Dougy Center to extend supportive services to the families, caregivers, schools, and the community.

We founded the Center on the belief that every child deserves the opportunity to grieve in a supportive and understanding environment. Based on that belief, we identified four basic principles for The Dougy Center.

- Grief is a natural reaction to loss of a loved one for children as well as adults.
- Within each individual is the natural capacity to heal oneself.
- The duration and intensity of grief are unique for each individual.
- Caring and acceptance assist in the healing process.

These principles have guided The Dougy Center since its early days, and continue to do so twenty-five years later.

A Visit from Elisabeth Kübler-Ross

The Dougy Center was blessed to have an official residence just a little more than two years after our first support group. We felt more independent; at last, we really were an official organization. Elisabeth had been an inspiration during those early years, so we asked her to join us for the official ribbon-cutting at The Dougy Center in February 1985. She agreed to come for the celebration as well as help The Dougy Center by giving a fund-raising lecture at the University of Portland. The event was held at the newly built Chiles Center, a domed facility for university athletic and con-vocation events. This was the only place we found that could hold, at a minimal cost, all of the people wanting to meet this world-renowned grief specialist. Nearly five thousand people attended, and it was standing room only. Elisabeth split the profit from this lecture with The Dougy Center, giving us $7,500. This was a life-saving gift at a time when we were trying to financially survive.

The next day, Bonnie Strauss from ABC's "Hour Magazine" was in Portland to do a story about the

Elisabeth Kübler-Ross attended the ribbon-cutting ceremony for the Warner Pacific House.

Bonneville Dam, but when she heard Elisabeth Kübler-Ross was in town she sidestepped the dam and let someone else cover that story. Bonnie and her crew met Elisabeth at The Dougy Center and they spent the entire day videotaping for a segment to be shown in April on "Good Morning America." This was the first national glimpse at the small and unknown children's grief support group in Portland, Oregon. This kind of national media exposure for The Dougy Center and our vision for

Elisabeth brought media attention to The Dougy Center.

helping grieving children was priceless.

In April 1985, the board of directors hired the first full-time employee at The Dougy Center. Jim Hussey became the Director of Volunteers, coordinating the volunteer program and recruiting and training new volunteers. He started the first official newsletter for The Dougy Center, *Bearhouse Chronicles*. Over the years Jim worked at the Center, he wore many hats—facilitator, newsletter editor, handyman, fund raiser, teacher, and public speaker. Volunteer facilitator Dean Conklin, who began working at The Dougy Center in 1985, wrote about Jim in the fall 1989 Newsletter:

> When I asked Jim for a message to the rest of us, he said, "I think the thing that I have, quote, 'learned' from The Dougy Center is that the volunteers there aren't healers. They are not there to heal people. They are there to heal themselves, to help themselves, and as long as they're there for that reason, the kids will be healed. But the minute they start trying to fix them or trying to heal them, they'll lose it. The message is stay aware of your own process. Stay aware of your own buttons that you pushed and your own weak spots and 'heal thyself.'
>
> In this same vein: "The facilitator is not the machinery, it's the oil that makes the machinery run smoothly. So your job is not to solve problems—just be oil."

Spreading the Word

The Dougy Center began receiving attention from Portland's news media in 1984, informing Oregonians about a program that most did not know existed. Reporters from *The Oregonian* wrote articles about the Center, and the regional television show, "AM Northwest," invited a six-and-a-half-year-old Dougy Center participant and me to be on the show. Additional local television and public service announcements helped get our message out to the community. However, the eight-minute segment on "Hour Magazine" gave The Dougy Center national attention. In July 1985, "ABC World News Tonight" with Peter Jennings ran a segment on The Dougy Center.

These nationally aired programs featuring The Dougy Center immediately resulted in requests from hundreds of people nationwide calling the Center asking, "What are you doing?" "How are you doing it?" "How can we do it in our community?"

In August 1985, we held our first National Training workshop that explained the vision of The Dougy Center. We offered firsthand experience in support groups for the five people who attended. Rachel and Paul Burrell attended our first workshop after the death of their eldest son. They realized there were no support groups for their other three children in Cincinnati, Ohio—or anywhere else, except for The Dougy Center. The Burrells started Fernside: A Center for Grieving Children in 1986. It became the second children's grief support program in the nation.

A reporter with the local PBS station, Marilyn Deutsch, developed a six-minute story on The Dougy Center that aired in February 1986 on Oregon Public Broadcasting's "Front Street Weekly." Ongoing local media exposure resulted in more interest from Portlanders who wanted to train to be facilitators—and, of course, more participants seeking support after a death in the family.

The print news media gave The Dougy Center consistent coverage from early on. One of the finest articles, and the one I cherish most, appeared in *This Week Magazine* in August 1986. (See page 120.) There was a cover photo of two-and-a-half-year-old Silas Quine sitting on my lap. The article, "The Fine Art of Caring" by Michael Burgess, included additional photos of children from The Dougy Center. Soon after, *The American Academy of Pediatrics News (AAP News)* published a two-page article on the Center, along with photos. I was thrilled to realize that the *AAP News* reached 34,000 pediatricians in the United States and Canada.

Bonnie Strauss at ABC continued to be interested in The Dougy Center. She had fallen in love with the program, and particularly with Jenny Richardson, a little girl whose story of loss moved Bonnie to tears. (See Jenny's story in Chapter Seventeen.) In July 1987, Bonnie returned to The Dougy Center to see how the program and Jenny were doing. She did a second story, a four-and-a-half minute segment for "Good Morning America."

After Bonnie's story aired nationally in July 1987, many more people contacted The Dougy Center seeking help to establish grief support groups in their communities. Urgent requests came from across the United States: "Please set up a workshop to train us to do what you are doing. There is such a need!"

That September we put on a far more polished National Training workshop than the first one in 1985. People came from across the nation—and when they went home new centers sprang up: The WARM Place for Grieving Children in Fort Worth, Texas, started by Peggy Bohme; the Center for Grieving Children in Portland, Maine, started by Bill Hemmens; and Bridges for Grieving Children in Tacoma, Washington, founded by Beverly Hatter; among others. Our national training sessions became longer and more professional as we learned more about helping grieving children. Today, this five-day program is called the "International Summer Institute," and draws participants worldwide who are interested in establishing programs for grieving children. (See Chapter Twenty, "The Dougy Center Today.")

The second National Training at The Dougy Center held in 1987.

More Support Groups

By the end of 1987, The Dougy Center had grown to eight evening groups for children, age six to eighteen, and eight corresponding parents' groups. After only five years the Center had served more than 3,200 children and parents. We never dreamed The Dougy Center would grow this rapidly.

Ongoing local and national television coverage inspired a growing number of people to contact The Dougy Center; they wanted to be trained in what we were doing or they were seeking help for grieving children. In March 1992, ABC's "20/20" showed a seventeen-minute segment about The Dougy Center with reporter John Stossel. Within five days after this show aired The Dougy Center received more than two thousand calls nationwide. Most of the callers wanted to know if there was a program in their area for their children.

Within the first five years we regularly had 110 children and 88 parents in ongoing groups. We had started more groups addressing different kinds of grief, many of them still functioning at the Center to this day.

There were two "Sons and Daughters" groups dealing with the death of parents; a new "Sibs and Friends" group for children who had experienced the death of a sibling or a best friend; a "Healing from Suicide" group that addressed the needs of children who had a parent or sibling die from suicide; "Healing from Violent Death/Homicide" for those healing from a violent death or homicide; and a group we called "Littles" for children age three to five who had a parent or sibling die. Each

The original "Sons and Daughters" group at The Dougy Center, which evolved from the first group of four children.

group had from eight to twelve children and at least four facilitators, except for the "Littles." This group needed to be smaller because of the children's young ages and their tendency to act out their grief rather than sit in a talking circle and talk. Many did not have adequate verbal skills to express what they felt inside. The "Littles" group was in great demand and continued to be unique in the U.S. and Canada at that time.

Jim Hussey (left) with a Dougy Center participant.

One of the top national experts in the area of death and dying was so astounded by our work with three-to-five-year-old children that he decided to visit The Dougy Center. Charles "Chuck" Corr, Ph.D., was a humanities professor at Southern Illinois University and was a member of The Dougy Center's Honorary Board. At the time he had already been involved with the publication of fifteen books on grief, as an author, co-author, or editor. I had met Chuck at an annual Association for Death Education and Counseling (ADEC) conference and we continued to connect annually at the ADEC conferences. Chuck decided to visit The Dougy Center and learn more about our work with young children. He took our volunteer training and was delighted to witness miracles at work. Chuck decided to include The Dougy Center in a research project he was working on at the time.

We added a special feature at The Dougy Center's Warner Pacific house after someone donated an eighty-pound punching bag. We anchored the bag to the water pipes at the bottom of the stairs in the basement. Izetta Smith thought it would be a great idea to have the punching bag for the children, noting, "Emotion equals commotion and motion." (See Chapter 15 for Izetta's story.) We adults named the punching-bag area the "Commotion Room." Before long, the children renamed it "The Volcano Room." The kids would line up to use the punching bag, jockeying to go first. We had to post facilitators nearby the punching bag to be sure all the children had an opportunity to have at the bag. They loved it. Eventually, when The Dougy Center moved to its permanent home, we created an actual room called "The Volcano Room," complete with padded walls, floor, ceiling, and punching bag.

A Permanent Home

By 1987, The Dougy Center had established itself in the local community as a place where children and their parents could find help for their grief. The house that had seemed more than adequate when we moved in was becoming crowded. After nearly four years we realized the small house on the campus of Warner Pacific no longer met the needs of so many children and their families. We were bursting at the seams with offices doubled up for staff, daily intake interviews with new potential participants, and practicum students observing at the Center.

As the groups expanded and the need for more support groups increased, we all began to look for a larger permanent home for the Center. One of our children's group facilitators, an older gentleman named Ralph Schwab, had his eye on a large, fixer-upper house with a huge yard in Southeast Portland. One day he walked up the front steps and knocked on the door. When the lady of the house, Beth Thorne, answered the door, Ralph stunned her by asking, "Have you ever considered selling your home? It is exactly the kind of home we are looking for."

This sizeable house had two stories and a full basement. Mrs. Thorne had been renting out three parts of the house as apartments, but at the time Ralph approached her about selling she had no renters. It took several months for Mrs. Thorne to decide that her house was truly too large for her. Finally she agreed to sell. This was an answer to our prayers. A price of $100,000 was finally agreed upon, and Mrs. Thorne gave us ten years to pay off the loan. The Chiles Foundation of Portland gave the The Dougy Center a $25,000 grant for our new home. That amount, plus a $5,000 donation from the Central East Rotary were huge financial boosts. We were on our way!

This beautiful old house was definitely a fixer-upper, but it held a promise for nearly three times as much space and a homeyness we wanted to provide for the families. Linda Usher and Sandy Bingham, now members of The Dougy Center's Board of Directors, pledged to do everything in their power to help. Through their creative efforts and hard work, they co-chaired the first "Hearts and Flowers Benefit" held at the elegant and historic Pittock Mansion in the West Hills of Portland. This black tie optional, fund-raising event featured desserts from Portland's finest restaurants, bakeries, and caterers. In addition, musicians played love songs from the past two centuries for entertainment. This event raised much-needed capital for the house. "Hearts and Flowers" has become an annual fund-raising event at The Dougy Center.

While writing this book, I asked Linda to share her thoughts about working with The Dougy Center. Linda was exuberant as she shared how The Dougy Center started out looking like a shaky proposition and moved on to become an international model for helping children deal with death. Recalling their efforts to raise money, Linda wrote:

> Because of the Hearts and Flowers event we were able to raise $10,000 for the house. By begging desserts, musicians, balloons, printing, and free public service announcement TV time, we were able to pull off a memorable event at the Pittock Mansion on Valentine's Day 1988. It was a grand success.
>
> Then it was time to fix up the house. Everybody was involved. We shamelessly abused our friends, families, and every appropriate

The house that became the permanent home for The Dougy Center.

business that could possibly help us. We were obsessed and our group absolutely committed. We burned a lot of midnight oil, manhandled (and womanhandled) paintbrushes, and exerted a lot of elbow grease. We used every bit of ingenuity we could muster. We even indulged in a bit of driving one day as we picked up a vehicle full of dozens of floor pillows in bright primary colors from an upholstery company. There was room in the car for the pillows, but no room for Sandy and me. Somehow we made it to the Dougy house.

The house was remodeled, flowers planted, the groups moved in, meals continued to be served, and children continued to heal. The Dougy Center family became our passion. Over the years the auxiliary has received far more from the center than they have given. We have become much more understanding of people who have suffered a loss; learning that "grief work" means work. We learned that there is no right or wrong way to react after a death. Healing takes time and our experiences as volunteers at The Dougy Center have helped us with the loss of our own parents and other people's losses around us.

We shall ever be grateful to The Dougy Center, to Bev, and to those who have followed. Of all the things and organizations and efforts the auxiliary has been involved with, we consider The Dougy Center to be one of the most memorable and life-affirming.

So many people stepped forward to help during those early critical years of The Dougy Center's formation. While writing the final chapters of this book, I found a sweatshirt in a box of mementos. It reads, "5th ANNIVERSARY - BPA" in a blue star. Below the star a line reads: "BPA'S Energizing the Community Benefit for The Dougy Center." The Bonneville Power Administration's 5th Annual Auction benefited The Dougy Center—another wonderful example of community organizations and individuals stepping forward to support our efforts.

Browsing through photos of Dougy Center events, I remember the carnival put on by Central East Rotary Group spearheaded by the same Ralph Schwab who found the Center's permanent house. He volunteered to be on the carnival dunk tank platform. We also held car washes, garage sales, and sold holiday wreaths, among many other events, to add to our coffers in those early days. Some of The Dougy Center children even donated their allowances to help out. The list of individuals, fund-raising events, and special angels is long.

The dream would never have materialized without the efforts of so many in the community. There was no money for anything for at least two years, so their services and donations were true blessings. Without this constant flow of blessings, I have my doubts that The Dougy Center, with all of its struggles to become, would have ever made it.

New Leadership for The Dougy Center

I served as The Dougy Center's Executive Director until February 1988, intensely involved with all aspects of its growth. However, after five-and-a-half years I realized I wanted to spend more time with the families at the Center and less time on administrative concerns. My new job title was Associate Director. I continued to work as a group facilitator—my greatest passion—being with the families and tending to the "heart" of the program.

In April 1988, the board hired Roselyn Meier as the second executive director of The Dougy Center. She had extensive experience with nonprofits, including serving as a vice president with regional YMCAs. At the time I wrote, "Roselyn's greatest strengths are my greatest weaknesses—board development, personnel management, administrative expertise and fund development." Roselyn stayed until December 1990, guiding the Center through difficult financial challenges and expanding services to the community. Among them was securing a two-year grant of $80,000 from the Murdoch Charitable Trust. This funding allowed The Dougy Center to create a children's grief support network among the twenty-six "sister programs" established at that time. This grant also allowed The Dougy Center to develop materials, including manuals and videos. In May 1990, The Dougy Center published the book, *I Wish I Were in a Lonely Meadow.* This book was for kids, by kids, in which the children shared their stories and artwork about a loved one's death by suicide.

For two years I worked with Donna Schuurman, a volunteer facilitator who joined The Dougy Center family in 1986. We worked as co-facilitators in the parents' "Healing from Suicide" group (now called "Healing from a Suicide Death"). Donna and I worked together extremely well, perhaps the most in tune I had ever been with another facilitator. Donna brought an intuitive wisdom as a facilitator that I greatly admired. She also showed a passion for and a commitment to The Dougy Center's work. During her time as a volunteer facilitator she conducted research for her doctoral dissertation titled, "The Impact of Parent Suicide on Children." Excerpts from her interviews with children at The Dougy Center were used in the Center's book, *I Wish I Were in a Lonely Meadow.*

Donna also served as a board member at The Dougy Center for four years, offering her strong business sense and great fund-raising abilities to build a firmer financial foundation for the Center. Previously, she had directed development and communications for several international relief and development organizations for twelve years. She also had worked with a consulting firm specializing in nonprofit organizations. After being a member of the Center's board of directors for several years, Donna became the third executive director in 1991. Prior to accepting the position, Donna had been the Director of Development for Pacific Crest Outward Bound School in Portland.

I continued to work as a group facilitator for a couple more years and was also the facilitator for the "Monthly Meeting" for families on waiting lists to join a support group. Bev Fulk had left the Center after about six years, and Izetta Smith moved on to her next life challenge after about nine years. In December 1990, I decided to pull back further, which coincided with my husband's diagnosis of bladder cancer. Allan's struggle with cancer consumed my daily life until his death in August 1993. After his death, I continued to volunteer at The Dougy Center, co-facilitating the "Monthly Meeting."

In December 1994, I decided to step back from my work as a facilitator, but have continued to stay connected with the Center to this day. In my July 1988 *Bearhouse Chronicles* column, "A Paws at Bev's Desk," I addressed the question, "Who is The Dougy Center?" I repeated this column in 1990 as I stepped back further. It summed up my feelings well. In part, this is what I wrote:

> I have frequently heard the statement, "You, Bev, are The Dougy Center." This has been said by board members, staff, volunteers, participants, and friends in the community.
>
> At first, when this is said, I feel greatly appreciated and it's like a pat on the back—a real boost to the ego. But always, directly following

the boost, other feelings bring me back to reality. Can you imagine what a burden it would be for one person to be The Dougy Center?

Let me share with you who I believe is The Dougy Center. I see The Dougy Center as a big family, growing larger and larger as families tend to do. Just because a participating family moves on to make closure from their group doesn't mean they are no longer a part of the family. And as volunteers move on to another place to serve, they, too, are still family members. It is the same with board members and staff.

… Being The Dougy Center is special for all of us—not just Bev Chappell. Being The Dougy Center is experiencing caring, safety, sharing, support, understanding and love. Being The Dougy Center is too great a burden for one person alone. We, The Dougy Center, must all continue to give and reach out to receive (right hand giving, left hand receiving) a constant circle of caring, support, and love. I invite each of you reading this article to take a rightful ownership of being The Dougy Center.

CHAPTER FOURTEEN

From Participant to Staff
Izetta Smith's Story

When I think about how The Dougy Center evolved, I think about the process of putting together a jigsaw puzzle. When you decide to put a jigsaw puzzle together, the picture on the box shows how the finished product is supposed to look. First you lay out the pieces on the table and turn them face up. Then, most people put the outside frame together. After the frame is completed, there are pieces waiting to find their places in the overall picture.

The puzzle, with its outside edges put together, and several clumps of pieces ready to add to the frame, is a bit like the early days of The Dougy Center. We had the main framework in place and one group that was meeting, but we certainly did not have a sense of the overall picture. In the beginning, The Dougy Center was trying to fill an ever-increasing need. We knew we needed to become more sophisticated, and trusted that we would figure out that part of the puzzle in time. Our first program director, Izetta Smith, played a key part in developing our vision for the children's grief support program. The program she developed in those early years became the basis for the program we use today.

Izetta first came to The Dougy Center with her son, Pan, after the death of his father in 1983. We had only started a grief support group for children about eight months before their arrival. Izetta began co-facilitating the parent group with Bev Fulk while she was still a participant. From the start, Izetta began making things happen, helping Bev and me develop the program that would be the foundation of The Dougy Center. I consider Izetta to be one of the pillars of this unconventional idea of children helping children grieve, offering us her

Izetta Smith and Allan Chappell

enthusiasm, hard work, and creativity at a time when we were piecing together this program.

To this day Izetta and I have remained good friends, and we are still very much in touch with the miracle of healing that continues at The Dougy Center and elsewhere. She was a lifesaver as well as a special friend while my husband struggled with cancer. She was a tremendous support to both of us as we all became aware that Allan was losing that struggle. Every Wednesday noon, before Izetta headed for work, she stopped by and she and Allan would play cribbage, a game Allan had taught her. And when Al was on so much pain medicine that he could no longer keep score, she sat with him and they sang silly songs. When he was confined to bed, she sat by Al's bedside and sang to him, or just held his hand. At Allan's memorial service Izetta sang "Farther Along" with many added verses that she had written just for Allan and our family. It was a beautiful tribute to Allan, and to our friendship. This kind of caring exemplifies who Izetta is, and the depth of her compassion. Izetta agreed to share her memories of those early years at The Dougy Center for this book. This is her story.

Izetta's Story

I was living in rural Oregon, re-orienting myself to a new career path after years as a professional theatre artist. Theatre work in 1980 had become too demanding and I began to be drawn toward work that was more "practical," something in the service of healing. Spontaneously, I thought, in the quiet of the Southern Oregon hills, that I could take my theatre skills and apply them as tools for helping traumatized children heal. When a fellow land-mate returned from San Francisco telling the tale of a woman, Arina Isaacson, who was using clowning skills in hospitals, I was immediately taken with the idea. I said, "That's it!"

I decided that first I must learn about illness, dying, and death, so I enrolled in an Elisabeth Kübler-Ross week-long workshop and headed for upper New York State. Elisabeth was an amazing teacher and I became quite devoted to her. Most amazing was that among the one hundred other students at the workshop was the very same woman-clown from San Francisco my friend had told me about. We became fast friends and I decided to do a month-long internship with her. My ten-year-old son, Pan, came with me for the holidays as I shadowed this inspiring clown-for-healing. When we returned, my son headed back to his father's home in Olympia, Washington, and I returned to Douglas County, Oregon. One month later Pan's father died instantly of a heart attack.

This death thrust me into a whirl-wind on many levels. I had decided to work with sick and grieving children, and suddenly I had a grieving child who needed my help. When I was ten my father had died, so I understood firsthand how it felt for a child grieving the death of a parent. What was I to do? I decided to write to Elisabeth. I knew she wouldn't remember me, but I also knew that she answered her mail. I wrote that I was in Olympia, Washington, living with my grieving son so he could finish his school year. What should I do?

Elisabeth wrote back, "Move back to Portland. Find Beverly Chappell. She is starting a center to help children who are grieving. Your son can get some help and you can help

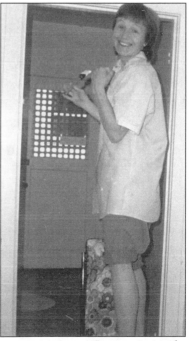

Izetta painting the
Warner Pacific house.

141

Beverly with the center." So, I moved back to Portland, a place where I had lived years before. I called Beverly Chappell and asked to meet her. When I arrived at her home, a neat one level house with an impeccable lawn, I dug out a butterfly puppet that I had made to resemble the one Arina had used in the hospitals. First I knocked, then put that butterfly puppet on my hand. The butterfly greeted Beverly when she opened the door, fluttering its bejeweled wings.

Immediately, I could see that Beverly was a visionary with dreams in her eyes and the courage to keep insisting that her vision come true. I understood that she needed someone to help lay the foundation of her dream. Elisabeth had sent me to her to help do this.

My Time at The Dougy Center

The first nine years of The Dougy Center were a time of immense creativity. People, volunteers, and staff came together to make a new form; to manifest a long-needed response to the needs of grieving children. When so few families came in the first year, we remembered Elisabeth saying repeatedly, "Go slow. Go even slower." So we went about the business of setting the structure of the support groups while the doctors, therapists and families watched to see if we were substantial enough to help the grieving children.

We developed a forty-hour training to prepare the volunteers for helping in the groups. We scheduled pre-meetings before each support group to prepare the volunteers for the afternoon or evening. In the early days, the support groups began with a pizza dinner for the families and volunteers, and then the parents and children would separate into their own groups. The evening ended with a closing circle: children, parents, volunteers, and staff together passing a hand-squeezed love around the circle. Then the staff and volunteers would have a post-meeting to discuss the evening's events.

The Dougy Center's first small group met for about a year while the Center's systems were developed. Then the groups took off like a brush fire, the demand for the service primed by the unmet needs of the families. Our job at the center for the next eight years was to catch up to the requests for our groups. Soon we had two groups, then four, then eight, then twelve. We had ten children, then twenty, then forty, then eighty, then one hundred.

We were always stretched to try things for the first time. As we laid the groundwork for how the center would function, we wondered: *How will the grieving children respond? Would the center be too sad a place?* No, the center was wild—wild with laughter and wild with the frenetic needs of the children to play out their grief. In those early days, we also questioned if the children wanted to talk about what happened. The answer was, "Well, yes and no." Children would talk, but often they would try to be compliant to our adult talking needs. Kids would sit for just so long before their needs to move, to externalize their feelings, drove them to do art or roughhouse and play.

I remember watching the opening circle on the in-house video, set up for me to review the groups each night. I would see the children, especially certain children, wiggle and rock, tease, and deflect the conversation. The facilitators, feeling obligated to keep the circle contained, would get annoyed by the children's commotion. When I saw this, I thought, *No! This commotion is the key. The commotion is part of a child's grief. Commotion is emotion in motion.*

Over time we developed a language to talk to the children as though their wiggling was not behavior to be disciplined. In fact, we realized this behavior was longing for another setting. At the bottom of

the stairway in the totally unfinished basement of the Warner Pacific house, we wrapped the plumbing pipes with foam and hung from these pipes an eighty-pound punching bag. During group meetings we invited the children who were too wiggly for the talking circle to go downstairs to the "Commotion Room"—a room the children quickly renamed "Volcano Room." Their grief, too, had a place to be expressed.

The punching bag in the Volcano Room

Years later, when we moved to our new and bigger house we created a grand Volcano Room with funds from the Central East Rotary Club. It had deep padding on all the walls, ceiling, and floor, plus punching bags, a gym mat, pillows, and stuffed bears. The Volcano Room became a soft, safe place to erupt! Children would emerge from the Volcano Room worn out, but we could hear them telling their parents as they were leaving the center that they couldn't wait to come back. We were surprised! How could children be so excited about coming to a grief center? We were so grateful to be meeting a need.

When inventing this new service for grieving children, our first goal was to do no harm. As we grew exponentially, this goal became more of a challenge. We understood that this kind of care required the watchful eye of an entire community. That is what we became—a community joined by grief.

Early on, I understood that each staff member, volunteer, parent and child had experienced grief. For some of us that grief was recent; for others it was distant. Some of us were at peace, some were not, but we all needed support for our stories. The Dougy Center community became a dynamic exchange of grief stories moving between participants, volunteers, and the staff. The children and parents were supported by the volunteers; the volunteers were supported by the staff; and the staff was supported by other staff.

Instead of having the pre-meetings for the purpose of analyzing group participants, I decided to have the meeting devoted to supporting the volunteers. In the early days, we began what we called a pre-meeting where we all could shift gears from what we had been doing to what we were about to do with the children and parents. This was one of the best ideas we had in those early days. We spent most of the hour going round the circle of volunteer facilitators, hearing about their own struggles, perhaps of the day and their work, or perhaps long standing and unmet emotional challenges that they had not felt safe to share before. Some of their struggles were re-stimulated by working with the grieving children and parents; and some were stimulated by life itself. At the end of this pre-meeting we were more aware of our humanness and vulnerability, which made us better prepared to be sensitive to the parents and children.

Also, from the beginning, even the staff meetings started with personal check-ins. The exchange with other staff about ourselves as people made our professional work so much more an act of cooperation. The Dougy Center was a place where we all wanted to be. It was a place of personal growth for all involved—not just for the children. It was quite amazing how our volunteers stayed on for years and grew as a community. To this day there are volunteers who have been with The Dougy Center more than twenty years.

Starting New Support Groups

One particularly difficult year when our support groups could in no way keep up with requests for placement in the groups, we came up with a creative solution. Our waiting list of families waiting to get into a support group was reaching forty, then sixty, then eighty families. We struggled with how we could ask grieving families to wait this long. Volunteers and staff came together and we decided to create a "Monthly Meeting" for the families that were on the waiting list.

The Warner Pacific house was extremely small. There was room for one parent group in the downstairs living room and one children's group in a downstairs bedroom. One tiny bedroom downstairs was a cramped office for both Jim Hussey and me. There were two larger bedrooms upstairs. One was Bev's office and the other was for the administrative assistant that we had for only a short time. We used that room for kids groups in the evening meetings. Occasionally, we would ask the Warner Pacific staff if we might use their gymnasium for a special evening when we combined groups. And sometimes, like when Tom Pinkson came to Portland, Warner Pacific College allowed us to use their auditorium.

The first "Littles Group"

So when we decided to do a "Monthly Meeting" for the people on the waiting list, we expanded into those areas that Warner Pacific kindly allowed us to use. As the "Monthly Meeting" grew larger, we found a new meeting place at the Sunnyside Adventist Church.

We had no idea if or how the "Monthly Meeting" would work, but so many volunteers asked to help that we felt the momentum to make these extra meetings work. Many rooms in the Warner Pacific College student center were filled with children, parents, volunteers, and staff. One particular "Monthly Meeting" around the holidays had one hundred participants. When we went to close the meeting with our traditional "love squeeze circle" the squeeze passed from hand to hand around a circle that lined a gymnasium-size auditorium!

Families continued to leave the groups being thankful. There were few complaints. We realized we were accomplishing our mission. Staff and volunteers were awed and humbled by the adventure. We learned that when we are really connected to one another, we create a webbing so strong that it can safely hold all kinds of trauma and hurt.

Soon, we saw the need to start groups for grieving children with special needs. In 1986 we started groups for children who had a sibling or best friend die. These groups were called "Sibs and Friends." When that specialty group was working well we had requests for us to do grief support for younger children. Because of parent requests, in February 1986, another group was started called "Littles" for three-to-five-year-old children who were grieving the death of a family member. At that time, the community assumption was that children this young could not possibly grieve. We did not know the answer to the special needs of these children. We knew that we did not know, but we were willing to try to learn. This willingness grew out of the strength of a cohesive community. Again, these little ones taught us what they needed to heal—*and they knew!*

Addressing requests from the community, in March 1988 The Dougy Center began a new group, "Healing from Suicide," for children who had a family member die by suicide. This was followed in November 1988 with a group called "Healing from Violent Death/ Homicide." This group was for children who had experienced those types of deaths in their families. There was no written information about these issues, so, again, we were in the act of invention.

A Lifetime Experience

The nine years that I spent at The Dougy Center were a very enriching part of my life, and I learned many things. I learned the foundation of the craft to which I am devoting the rest of my life as a therapist for ill and grieving children and their families. I also learned that when we work together in community we work at our fullest potential. There were other vital things learned, too: that the key to a cohesive group is to know each other's stories and struggles, and that leadership is best when it isn't that visible. I always admired Bev Chappell's leadership because

Donna Schuurman, Bev Chappell, and Izetta Smith.

she asked me to follow my instincts and my heart and then she thanked me profusely for all that I did. It was my aspiration to do the same. Forty or so people made The Dougy Center come into being. My greatest learning was that I was most useful not trying to be the source of inspiration, but recognizing and encouraging the inspiration of others.

It was truly thrilling to be a part of an historic time when our culture, and soon the international community, changed its perspective about children's grief. It was an honor to be a pioneer translating into words what the grieving children were showing us about their needs. It is a great gift, even today, when I hear of The Dougy Center helping to train people from all over the world, to know that I have contributed to the lessening of children's pain and grief.

Recently, when I saw the videotape of the woman from Rwanda who is opening a Dougy program in that country I was inspired. My heart filled with tears of hope realizing she was creating a healing center in her country for children orphaned by genocide. Of course, in the very same moment my hopeful heart was washed with the cold reality about how much more we have to do to protect our children.

CHAPTER FIFTEEN

The Tumbler of Life

Arock tumbler and three ten-pound tumbler barrels have been common fixtures in our home since the early 1960s. I had been drawn to collecting interesting rocks since I was a child, looking for unusual rocks near the Iowa River that flowed through our small town. When my mother returned from her trek to the post office each day, she would often be holding a handful of pretty rocks that she had gathered on her walk. Her fascination with rocks soon became mine as well.

When my husband, Allan, and I moved to the Pacific Northwest I fell in love with the rugged Oregon coast, especially as a Midwestern transplant. Having grown up in Camas, Washington, Allan was thrilled that I soon came to love the ocean and beaches as much as he did. One Sunday we happened to wander into a dilapidated rock shop on the south end of Lincoln City and met the owner, a crusty older woman with a generous heart, who taught us all about rocks. During the course of many visits to the coast and this rock shop, I became a rock hound.

From the time our two children were toddlers, we combed the beach for agates and jasper, already half polished by the ocean's power and the gritty sand. Kathy and Steve were excited to help their parents find polishable rocks, and they learned at an early age which ones to put in their pockets and which ones to leave on the sand. Before long, our two-year-old son, Steve, could spot an agate even while riding high on his daddy's shoulders.

Over the course of frequent visits to the Oregon coast, we would gather rocks by the handfuls. It was a great family hobby. Although the whole family helped to find those elusive agates, I was the rock hound who did something with them once we got home. When there were enough rocks to fill a barrel for tumbling, the lengthy process would begin. The rocks tumbled in the ten-pound barrels nonstop for four months before they were smoothed. Then I took them out of the barrels, thoroughly washed them, and then put them back in the barrels along with polishing powder to tumble for another week.

Finally, the rocks tumbled in a detergent for two or three days to wash off all of the powder and make them sparkle. Only after this long process did we display the brilliantly colored and uniquely patterned stones in jars or baskets for all to enjoy. Visitors to our home were invited to take stones as keepsakes if they so desired. I understood that not everyone was into rocks as much as I was.

Little did I know those years of tumbling rocks would become a metaphor for working with grieving children and their families, and understanding the unfolding of their grief on their way to healing.

An Epiphany

On September 7, 1985, my husband and I celebrated our thirty-third wedding anniversary at the Oregon coast. We had driven to Road's End, our usual tradition while at the coast, to see if there were any rocks on that part of the beach. Allan decided to drive back to the condo, park the car, then walk the beach back to meet me. It was an unusually warm, sunny day with little or no wind. I tied my sweater sleeves around my waist and began to walk, scanning the shoreline for the right kind of rocks.

When Allan caught up with me, I had a handful of small agates, and red and yellow jaspers. We walked together silently, each of us immersed in our own thoughts as our eyes stayed peeled for the always-elusive agates. At one point, I stopped, completely absorbed by my handful of rocks. Allan walked back to me and asked, "What did you find?"

Thinking aloud, I replied, "Here I have a handful of rocks in my right hand—the here and now, the known and the conscious. They are in my hand because I know of their potential to be polished and to become shiny; to become, in a sense, gems. The left hand is the future—the unknown, the unconscious. Perhaps the left hand will hold the finished product, the gemlike stones."

I rubbed the rocks between my hands, absorbing the sensation of their wetness and the gritty sand. Still thinking aloud, I added, "And in between the potential of the dull, rough rocks with cracks and scratchy edges, and the final gems, must be the brutal action of the rocks with coarse grit and water in the tumbler. The rocks bang and hit against each

149

other and in the process get sanded down—smoothed, rounded, and polished—by the action within the tumbler. They are bumped around in the tumbler, like we are as we tumble through life with our knocks, pain, disappointments, losses, and hardships. Some of the rocks will disintegrate and mix with the grit, never to become those smooth gems. Some of the softer ones will crack in the tumbling process. But most of them will polish and become things of beauty. It is rough treatment and it is painful, but oh, to be a gem!"

The *Aha* of that insight was exciting. Allan recognized the epiphany as well. He put his arm around me as he usually did when we walked the beach together, my right hand still filled with the rocks. We walked along the ocean's edge for a long time in silence. Then an even more profound thought hit me: *I wonder if God walks the beach of life, selects the people He sees with potential and polishes them in the tumblers of their lives. He mixes the pain, hurts, losses, and frustrations (the grit) and tears (the water) to create people who could "emerge from their tumbler" and very well be "gems." If that is true, it would make life's hardships more bearable as we move through them on our way to our "gem role."*

This whole process of tumbling rocks to polish them is not easy on the rocks. They are smoothed by battering against each other for a lengthy period of time. Similarly, the process of easing grief is also lengthy and many times a great struggle. It appeared to me that the two processes were quite parallel. Perhaps that is why it is called "grief work."

Elisabeth Kübler-Ross had a favorite saying that echoes my thoughts about the tumbler of life each of us must experience:

> Should you shield the canyons
> from the windstorms,
> you would never
> see the beauty of their carvings.

Polished Rock Ceremony of Closure

After we moved The Dougy Center to its first home on the campus of Warner Pacific College I came to feel that it was not right to have the child participants make closure with the group and just leave, walk away empty-handed with nothing to show for their time and energy spent at the Center. Many times I asked myself, *What would make that time be remembered, perhaps even as valuable, to the child making a closure? What might remind them of all of the hard work they had done, tears they had shed, and the pounding they had done on the punching bag in the basement?*

The answer finally came: When a child completes at The Dougy Center give him or her *polished rocks!* The difficult rock tumbling process mimicked what happened to the children and their families as they attended support programs, tumbling through their pain and tears, finally coming to a place of healing.

So, shortly after we started our first "Sons and Daughters" group at Warner Pacific, we began the Rock Ceremony. When a child notified us that she or he would be leaving the group in two weeks—we required the participants to give us a two-week notice—I would put together some polished rocks in a piece of Saran Wrap and tie it with a pretty strip of yarn. (In time, colorful fabric drawstring pouches replaced the piece of Saran Wrap.) Included among all the shiny polished rocks was one rough rock to symbolize the rough path the child had trod to reach this point of closure, and to symbolize the grief that would always remain a part of him or her.

The Rock Ceremony held monumental significance for the children, especially the inclusion of a rough rock. Once or twice I forgot to include a rough rock while assembling the package. When the child realized a rough rock was missing, we had to scurry out to the gravel driveway and find just the right rough rock to include in the package.

When the child making the closure received the package of rocks, she or he would take them out of the pouch, hold them, and carefully look at each rock. Then the child passed each rock from child to child around the circle. The children participating in this closing circle would get the opportunity to look at and hold these rocks in their hands, rubbing them together, and wondering in their own hearts if they were approaching the time when they would be ready to leave the support group.

This closure ceremony must have made a powerful impression on the kids, because even now, many years later, some of those children who are now adults will tell me they still have their pouch of polished rocks in a very special place in their home. These rocks, which I like to think are symbols of their time at The Dougy Center, are still prominent in their thoughts—and in their hearts. The Rock Ceremony continues to be a ritual at the Center to this day.

CHAPTER SIXTEEN

The Dougy Center Mural

Ann Hinds came to The Dougy Center in the mid-1980s as a volunteer facilitator. At the time, Ann faced the imminent deaths of friends in a community rife with AIDS. She spent her first two years at The Dougy Center co-facilitating a "Sibs and Friends" group with Izetta Smith. She helped start a new children's group for child survivors of a death by murder, and was a facilitator with that group for another three years.

As a visual artist, Ann brought many talents to The Dougy Center, using art activities to help the children process their grief. As a community organizer, her talents for working with groups of people made her a natural for heading up the mural project at the Center, working with many different children facing many stories of loss and grief. In the end, Ann developed the original idea for a mural far beyond what anyone could have imagined. Her dedication to the children and the accurate expression of their loss and grief through visual art remains a lasting legacy at the Center today. For years, children have drawn solace and inspiration from the mural, and I am sure generations to come will benefit from Ann's efforts on behalf of The Dougy Center Mural. Here is Ann's story.

E. Ann Hinds' Story

Over the course of two years, I met and worked with two hundred children, to create a 144-square-foot mural in the basement of The Dougy Center. The artists ranged in age from four to nineteen years old.

Every image concerns the death of someone important to the artist: a mother or father, brother or sister, friend or relative.

I had worked for three years with children's support groups as a volunteer facilitator at The Dougy Center when Program Director Izetta Smith showed me a delicate drawing by Sean Fields. The winged figure represented his time at the Center. Staff wanted the image painted onto a wall as a statement of children's grief, but I envisioned a mural that would reveal an even bigger picture. By the Spring of 1989, I discovered exactly how complex this idea could become!

The available wall was downstairs in the basement of The Dougy Center. I thought, *This mural will never see the light of day!* But sitting next door to what we called the Volcano Room—where children physically raged against padded walls and floor, or pummeled a punching bag—I realized the mural could be an emotional investment in the literal foundation of the center. I found a tiny, Jungian, trapdoor in the wall that accessed the water main. With that discovery, I became convinced it was the perfect place. For me, the water main proved an insight about human process. Being 98% water, we need to flush our emotional plumbing on a regular basis to stay healthy. That the Center's water main would be integral to the mural was, in metaphor, the powerful potential of the basement. Now it needed a child's eye view.

The Children as Artistic Directors

Young people attending The Dougy Center ranged in age from "The Littles" (pre-schoolers) to the "Teens," some already out of high school. Participants represented a complex configuration of needs, ideas, peer systems, individual personalities, circumstances, and losses. Each one occupied a niche in this children's community of grief.

In preparation, I attended every Dougy support group for four visits. I spent time with all 200 children. We met in clusters, pairs, and one-on-one. I described my intentions to integrate their individual offerings into one big painting. I explained how I would replicate their work in paint, promising to be as accurate as possible. Many decided not to contribute to the mural, but others were excited by the proposition, grabbing crayons and pencils and returning with hands full of rumpled pictures. Some worried, asking questions: "Were good memories of the person who had died the best? Or could they illustrate their pain and rage?"

I assured them that every manifestation was acceptable and promised to be true to whatever they offered—*nothing* would be rejected. For children who didn't trust their own skills in imaging emotions, I offered to be their hands. I suggested they be the "art directors," describing what they wanted to represent them, and trusting my adult skills to produce it. One youngster came with a page from a *National Geographic Magazine* saying, "Can you copy this *exactly?* This picture of the doe and the fawn? And can you put the mother over here and the baby over there? I want them to be separated, just *this* far apart," she explained by holding up her hands to show me the exact spacing.

Reflecting on the process, I wonder now at my openness and trust; but there was guidance in that basement—the presence of love and cooperation. Children visited me as I worked, stopping to check on my progress on their way to the Volcano Room or to play pinball. We discussed specific sketches tacked to the wall, using the same guidelines of respecting confidentiality that they used in their support groups. I shared the names of children or meanings of their drawings only with prior permission. We respected the boundaries of The Dougy Center; agreeing to the guidelines and the sense of safety they offered.

I wanted a painted wall added into the mural to symbolize barriers and breakthroughs, to provide a place for "The Littles" to put their marks, and for graffiti work from teenagers. Steven Keenan, a friend and fellow volunteer at Cascade AIDS Project, himself a painter, agreed to help. He painted bricks with a sensitive combination of realism and a style suited to the children's designs.

The mural holds both the regression and the progress of bereaved children healing, morphing through every phase of human development. The painted wall breaks open to a passageway of paved stones. It recalls the shiny and the unpolished stones Bev Chappell gave each child upon "graduation."

On the painted brick wall, side-by-side, are handprints of the preschoolers, footprints of the middle-schoolers, and the spray paint of a high schooler. An orange basketball bounces at the front of the opening, echoing the globe of gold, the ancient egg-like orb, symbol of all beginnings in a universal visual tongue.

Working with the Children

My education included training in creative arts and emotional work. I had also experienced death directly and by proximity, as a courtroom illustrator for TV news, where I had become familiar with many families surviving a murder loss. As a volunteer facilitator at The Dougy Center for five years (including the two years creating the mural), I had worked with the "Sibs and Friends" group the first three years; then the "Healing from Murder" group for another two. The last year I worked at The Dougy Center as paid, on-call, staff. This allowed children to get to know me and build trust over time.

The familiarity of my presence allowed them to express themselves more openly during the mural project. I realized I needed to be accountable for accurately representing each child's artwork in the mural. Each needed to be able to bring a trusted friend or family member down to the basement, and point to a spot on the wall and say with full authority, "That one is mine!"

I had many ways to build trust with the children. One was a method of reflective listening I used when the kids played outside. I would shout out the "play by play" like a sportscaster, describing what each child was doing as she or he did it. They were exhilarated to hear their names called out aloud, and to have an adult simply notice and acknowledge their movements.

> Tanya is headed toward the swing set with amazing speed;
> Johnny is climbing up the slide backwards;
> Suzy is chasing Darryl with a Frisbee in her left hand;
> Tony and Timmy are wrestling on the ground by the tool shed.

This playful narration allowed them to feel "real." It affirmed their existence and trajectories. In assessing the accuracy of my observations, they became more trusting of my ability to see and hear. As a result, they disclosed more when their energy subsided and they were back inside; and especially when we worked together on the mural.

Some landscapes had clouds with sad expressions hidden in their depths. I didn't see those faces at first. They appeared only as I transcribed the drawings into paint. I worked to draw each cartoon on the wall exactly as the young people had expressed themselves on paper. I didn't want to illustrate my own assumptions or to interpret things that

Linda Kliewer ©1990

Ann Hinds working on the 144-square-foot mural.

"seemed obvious" to me. I needed to retain the original emotional content present in their "unconscious" visual expression. In that way, the children's designs began to speak.

Sad and angry faces emerged from clouds, or the foliage of a child's tree. At those moments of insight I gasped with comprehension—it wasn't just a cloud crying rain, there was a picture embedded in the picture. I saw self-portraits of distressed children emerge from the sky of the mural—bearing a message for all to see.

Time spent in self-expression revealed and released confusion. The images could "talk back" to each creator in his or her own artful language. The "words" of line, color, and light appeared in every picture they offered to the mural's design. Through seeing what they had to say, children were able to come to terms with their own stories.

One staff member introduced me to a nine-year-old girl who had never wanted to make art during her visits to The Dougy Center. She said she only saw things in black and white after her mother died. But she was willing to work with the two of us on a piece for the mural. As she created a memorial to her loss, drawing a picture of positive memories, she told us it was the first time she had seen color since her mother had died. She told us, "The light is slowly coming back into my life."

There was a young man whose family members died in a plane crash. His contribution to the mural was a picture of a lizard with rows of zigzag lines running down its back. I thought it an interesting design element, but I didn't understand the relevance until his brother persuaded him to tell the story. He had once seen a lizard crushed under the tires of a bulldozer. The zigzag lines were the tread of a huge tire, impressed in the flattened lizard's back. It had been a stark experience of death, and the image came to him in representing his loss. As I reflected the impact of his drawing, the intensity of his emotional release was palpable—so powerful that he requested I use a *different* design for the mural. He couldn't draw it himself, not because he couldn't draw, but because he couldn't bear to. He gave me explicit instructions, describing how the lizard looked in life, prior to being run over by the bulldozer. He told me what immature lizards looked like, and how their colors and patterns changed as they grew to adulthood. He wanted me to represent that lizard as an explicitly intact adult.

A truism in grief work is that every new grief restimulates other unresolved losses. One elementary school boy from the "Healing from Murder" group, which I co-facilitated, used art when he came to deal with the death of his grandmother. He had a great need to throw paint. But he only wanted to fling and spatter it, like a young Jackson Pollack. He didn't use a brush, or create an image. Every meeting I set up a painting space so he could stand back and throw the paint. Knowing that using his arms and upper body helped to open his lungs, and that this activity helped him to breathe and grieve, I was happy to mask the walls and provide him with supplies and support.

During our post-meetings, we facilitators expressed concerns that his activity spanned weeks without him specifically addressing his grandmother's death. In addition, he required more one-on-one time with facilitators than other children, and he didn't want to interact with peers. This boy was unable to put words to his experiences; yet his emotions were intense and his facial expressions reflected great inner turmoil. What eventually surfaced was that he had been sexually abused during the time frame of his grandmother's murder. His need to grieve through painting was a part of *that* healing process as well. Painting freed him to tell his mother about the sexual abuse. Once he was able to explain the extenuating circumstances of his grief, he lost his interest in painting and joined in activities with the other children. Eventually, he contributed a representational piece for the mural regarding his grandmother's death.

I was often amazed and humbled by the imagery children chose to express their grief or their love for a family member who had died. The bouncing basketball, representing one boy's grief expression, was also a profound memory: his father died of a heart attack while playing basket-ball. In another image, water flows across the upper left-hand corner of the mural, past a volcano, where a wave strikes a hillside. This depicts a specific connection: "My grandmother and I liked watching the water hit the hillside. That was our thing."

A tan-colored dog and three stick people with deathly white faces stand together on a grassy hillside in the upper right quadrant of the mural. While creating his drawing, the artist explained that at the moment of learning of the death "it felt like being attacked by a large, vicious dog. Then shock. Then sorrow."

Some of the children drew chaotic circles in multiple colors, expressing "feelings all mixed together." I had seen work like this by adults who could put words to the experience. They said it felt like they were literally going in circles. A huge component of grief is confusion. And the scrambling of colors spoke to me of a disorganized spectrum of physiological and human attributes, like energy systems represented in the Hindu Chakra color spectrum, the colors mixed at random by deep loss.

One six-year-old boy had trouble talking about his family's loss. He couldn't say who had died, even in Opening Circle. Instead, he pleaded incessantly to go to the playground, talking of nothing but riding the merry-go-round. Despite our admonitions to slow down, and our warnings against harming himself, he would, without fail, push the merry-go-round too fast, and "accidentally" fall off and hurt himself. He would then let one of us hold and comfort him. All the grief of the death seemed to suddenly flood out of him.

Linda Kliewer (left) and Barbara de Manincor
assist in transferring children's designs to the mural wall.

I could see similar responses in some of the children during the visits to support groups prior to collecting imagery. There were many who could not put words or images to their feelings; kids who scribbled and drew and ripped up the pieces—the process of externalizing rage or fear through their agitated movements seemed an end in itself. Nothing they created could represent their pain, and words wouldn't work. The art supplies afforded them a release process with no product left to archive their feelings.

Helpers

Initially, I had hoped more kids would paint directly on the wall. But in reality, there were fewer than a half dozen who were willing to do that. One teenager, an excellent graffiti artist, had to work with spray paint. It was obvious he would paint his message himself. His need to do graffiti justified the brick wall within our mural: the representation of a "built surface" providing a context for the graffiti.

In the beginning, I had also hoped that one or two of the Dougy participants would fall in love with the painting process and volunteer to assist me. In imagining helpers, I had not counted on the magnitude of grief in every submission. I soon realized no child had the capacity to work on another's picture of bereavement. Each one's grief was as much as could be borne. The challenge was far more than making a transcription of a design, it also required transcribing the inherent emotions.

So, I recruited artistic friends, many of whom had attended the grief trainings I provided for Cascade AIDS Project. They were familiar with the precepts of active listening and grief process. It often took more effort convincing others to help me paint than it did to paint alone. After an evening or afternoon at the wall, they usually had done all they could, and I ended up painting over 90% of the mural with direction from the children.

Acutely aware that our work at The Dougy Center provided a "cutting-edge" service, I knew this mural broke ground for an incredibly important movement in peer support for young people. A "must do" kind of feeling persisted in my gut during the two years working on the mural. Growing up with so many of my own childhood losses, this opportunity to use art to assist children in dealing with their emotional distress was a way for me to learn while creating a precedent for a new generation that had not been available in mine. I simply felt compelled to follow through, whatever the cost, and despite what seemed at times like an endless project.

The Mural in Self-Reflection

The inherent grief of this mural affected *me* greatly. I channeled the emotions of many deaths grieved in a community of 200 youngsters onto a single surface—using my own left arm and acrylic paint. The grief went through me physically, not always coming out intact. Bits remained inside me, magnetizing my own losses, developing into knots in my neck and shoulder muscles. My own unfinished grief mixed with the losses of others. It was a challenge to understand and come to terms with "psychic hygiene" and emotional boundaries. Throughout the creation of the mural, I was fortunate to have others supporting my emotional process as I worked to distinguish my feelings from the feelings of the children, and in turn, the feelings they carried for their families.

This was especially difficult when, halfway through painting the mural, my only nephew died of a drug overdose. My family of origin was in crisis and disarray. In addition, this was Oregon during a political climate of hate crimes and the castigation of sexual minorities, which directly affected me and my partner, as well as family and friends. And, I was witnessing the death march of AIDS through my community.

My other volunteer work, training non-professionals to serve as practical and emotional support counselors, continued at Cascade AIDS Project. My day job was producing a bi-weekly Lesbian and Gay community newspaper—filled with stories of bias, condemnation, and stigma. Apart from the mural, times were difficult.

And still, I learned from and with the children. It was a constant inspiration and reminder of the durability of the soul and the burdens one can sustain with sufficient support. The kids worked individually and collectively, often without any other resources or support from churches, schools or neighbors. They endured, and returned time after time, to face their feelings; trusting that all of us at the Center would be there for them—that they would not be left alone, left out, or left behind. That love and belonging, so essential to mending hearts, was there for me as well: for my past and present losses.

Completing the Mural

I worked across the entire surface of the wall for the duration of the painting process. Once images were accounted for, painted on in their chosen spots, recorded, and checked off my list, I went back in with smaller brushes and the original sketches to check for accuracy of detail. I took tiny pots of leftover paint for the background to touch up areas for smoother transition; painting from one segment to another until everything flowed as seamlessly as possible.

And as my own closure, I painted a dedication to my nephew Daman Mahler. Inside the little trapdoor to the water main, I expressed my own loss, which had been a guiding force in bringing the project to an end. When I finished the last stroke of the mural, I sat quietly with the wall, and cried. I meditated and sent out "Invoices to the Universe:" blessings for those who died, for those who grieved, for those who contributed, for those to come.

When the mural was complete, I checked in with the children still attending The Dougy Center, asking if they felt accurately represented; if they were satisfied with their individual contributions; and whether they felt the wall "worked" as an overall statement. I was hugely relieved to receive nothing but smiles and nods from the kids. They all seemed content it was done.

The Dougy Center staff had been very patient with my turning the basement into an art studio. I spent many hours tracking the original pieces, making sure each child was accounted for; and designing the complex relationships of content and composition. I often wondered whether

LINDA KLIEWER

Donna Schuurman and Ann Hinds looking at the mural book.

the disparate puzzle pieces would add up to a coherent whole. In the end, they did, and the mural was officially completed April 21, 1991. The children had tremendous pride in this collective statement for The Dougy Center, as well as in their individual paths of grief and healing.

They had come to understand that by leaving a statement of grief on the wall, surrounded by the shared but individual experiences of all the other children, they would also help those to come. And, whether the message was of loved ones in happier times, of personal suffering, or simply a family in disrepair, the images would stand as beacons of knowledge, long after the artists of the mural had gone.

The mural tells every new child facing serious loss, "You do not suffer alone; other young people have blazed a trail." All of us at some time in a bereavement wonder, "Will I ever get through this? Is there a light at the end of this tunnel?" Our mural depicts that sad trail: through emptiness, anger, confusion, and doubt. This mural also stands as a children's shrine to hope and healing within a supportive and loving community.

After finishing the mural, I constructed an oversized book with all the names of participating children and a map to match a grid painted on the wall that enables one to locate specific work. The book includes photos of adults and children engaged in different stages of the work, as documented by Linda Kliewer. Some of the children's original artwork is also included in the book along with my notations telling stories of the artists' processes and reasons for the imagery they chose.

The process of creating the wall was a healing experience for all who participated. Anyone who has ever suffered a loss will relate to some portion of this mural. The wall continues to speak to grieving children about where they have been, where they are, and where they may be headed. There is agony and beauty and success available here. This mural is a teaching aid for those in grief: a map for reorienting one's life in the wake of loss. It is an archive of survival.

CHAPTER SEVENTEEN

A Portrait of a Family in Grief

T here are many families who could write their stories about death and grief and they might parallel this family's story. Many have come to The Dougy Center and found what they call "a safe, warm nest" where they could begin to heal. I have seen so many families come to their first meeting at the Center looking terribly frightened of even being in the building. Then, after two or three meetings their sad faces begin to show smiles and an occasional laugh. When they find others in the same situation, they realize they are no longer alone in facing a new world of grief. Witnessing this wonderful transition always puts a smile on my face as I compare the "thens" (when they arrived) and the "nows" (as they are leaving the program).

The following three stories come directly from a family who felt the forces of death when they least expected it—at a time when this family's life was beautiful and serene. The Richardson family included the parents, Laurie, thirty-three, Doug, thirty-six, and their children, Jenny, six and a half years old, and Patrick, three and a half years old. Suddenly, their lives were turned upside down when Doug, a train engineer, died in a tragic accident at work.

The first story in this portrait of a family in grief is through the eyes of Jenny, who wrote about her father's death for a school assignment about six years after he died. Later, we printed her story in one of the early newsletters at The Dougy Center. In 2006, I had the great fortune of receiving a letter from Jenny talking about how the The Dougy Center helped her when she was a grieving child as well as her ongoing journey through grief as an adult. Laurie Richardson also shares her story of how she and her children benefited from The Dougy Center, and how she went on to become a volunteer at the Center. I also included recent reflections by Patrick, now a young adult, who was only three at the time of his dad's death.

As of 2007, some twenty thousand family members have walked through the doors of The Dougy Center, each with his or her own story of death and grief. This is the story of one family's journey.

Jenny Richardson

Sunday, January 1, 1984, is a day I will never forget. On that day I lost the innocence, beauty, and security of childhood. I was forced into a world of fear, insecurity, sadness, and tears.

I woke up on that cold foggy morning to my mother's soft voice and tear-stained face. She quietly said, "Jenny, do you know what heaven is?"

"Yes," I replied, "That's where you live with God."

"And there is no pain," my mom added. "Well, Jenny, Daddy had an accident last night. He was hurt very badly. Now he is in heaven with God." Then Mom began to cry and cradled me in her arms.

"How long does he have to stay there?" I asked. "When will my daddy come home?"

"Never," Mom told me. Although I knew something was terribly wrong, I just didn't want to believe it.

The next few days were a maze of activities; lots of people coming in and out, television cameras, newspaper reporters, flowers and other gifts arriving, and food for meals we didn't feel like eating.

As days went by, the story began to unfold for me. It was a foggy night; the bridge tender did not see my dad's train coming and opened the bridge for a sailboat. The bridge derailer was broken and the bridge tender forgot to check the track. Because of this seemingly small error, two men were trapped in a train engine at the bottom of the Willamette River, leaving four children fatherless. This was the beginning of my journey through the grieving process.

The Richardsons, 1985.

164

The first few months after my dad's death are a blur. I remember lots of tears, sleeping in my mom's bed, never staying home, and hiding in awkward places at school. It was hard to be a part of a world that I felt I didn't belong in. Nobody I knew had lost their dad. I was beginning to realize I had.

The pain of this loss was becoming unbearable. Not only had I lost my dad, but I felt like I was losing my mom, too. She couldn't cook or clean, she just wandered around aimlessly and cried all the time. For days, she didn't get out of bed. I was afraid that she was going to leave me, too.

Just when the storm of my life seemed the darkest we found a glimmer of light—The Dougy Center. This place became a calm in the center of my stormy life. Beverly Chappell started this support center for grieving children and their parents. Bev is a special lady who believes that every child deserves the opportunity to grieve in a supportive and understanding environment, even though our society often fails to understand the needs of a child or a family in grief.

The Dougy Center welcomed my family and me with open, loving, and healing arms. We went to meetings there every other Wednesday night. Our evenings began with a potluck dinner, then the parents would go into the living room with the adult facilitators and the kids would go into the playroom with the children's facilitators. We began with an

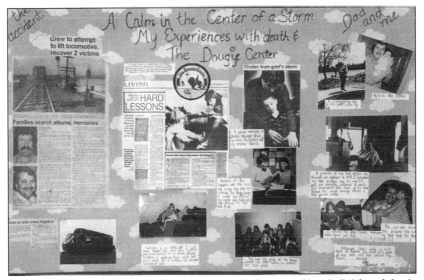

Jenny's school project tells the story of her dad's life and death.

opening circle and then moved into different activities that satisfied our own needs.

I loved my time at The Dougy Center. I soon found that if I shared my pain with others who had losses like mine, they helped me to feel more comfortable when they talked about the people in their life who died, and I talked about what happened to my dad.

The mission of The Dougy Center is to provide loving support in a safe place so children grieving a death can share their experiences and go through the healing process. The Dougy Center program operates on these principles:

- Grief is a natural reaction to the loss of a loved one for children as well as adults.
- Within each individual is the natural capacity to heal oneself.
- The duration and intensity of grief are unique for each individual.
- Caring and acceptance assist in the healing process.

During my two years of bi-weekly meetings at The Dougy Center, it became my family's lifeline. The people at the Center were like my family because they were the only ones who could listen and understand. My relatives could not understand or help because they were dealing with their own pain.

In September 1986, I finally decided I could leave the Center with a promise from Bev that I could help other children in some way who had also suffered a loss. On my last night, I was presented with a bag of beautiful polished rocks containing one rough stone. Bev had collected and polished these rocks herself. The stones that were shiny represented the healing that had taken place in my life. The one remaining rough stone is a reminder that although I have healed, I will still always carry with me some rough edges and pain throughout my life. My dad was a very special man. My rough rock is a symbol that there is a part of me that will always hurt, and I know I can expect it. This is okay because I will be able to deal with it.

My experiences with The Dougy Center and Dad's death have opened a door for my future. I am now making choices that will affect my future. I spend extra time working with children who have lost a loved one. I plan to make psychology a part of my future in order to help children who have had an unbearable loss in their life. I can support others through their private grief.

I have had some wonderful experiences because of The Dougy Center. I have met many wonderful people, been allowed to participate in grief workshops, talked to high school kids about death and grief, and facilitated in the center's "Monthly Meeting." Although Dad's body is not here on earth, his soul is a part of me and will live within my heart forever.

Recently, Jenny wrote me the following letter about her father's death and her experiences at The Dougy Center. Since then, Jenny and her husband, Matt, were blessed with a baby girl, Natalie, born March 1, 2007.

I am now thirty years old, yet that heart-broken little girl is still a part of me and always will be—and that is okay. This is what The Dougy Center is all about; through the love and kindness of its facilitators we learn to take that heartbreak and through lots of talking, playing, and drawing, we turn it into comforting memories of the ones we love.

I am lucky now to follow in Bev's footsteps as a nurse and also take what I learned at The Dougy Center and pass it on to bone marrow transplant patients in my nursing career. If I can touch any of them the way Bev has touched so many of our lives, I will consider myself a success.

Just two years ago, I faced a day that I have been both anticipating and dwelling upon since Dad's death; my wedding day. Even as a little girl, one of my first revelations after Dad's death was that I would not have a father to give me away on my wedding day. I remember being heartbroken by the image of walking down the aisle by myself toward my future. This past year when the fateful day finally came, I found myself strangely at peace without Dad's physical presence. As my brother escorted me down the aisle toward my husband, I could feel Dad there with me. I was not alone.

Since my time at The Dougy Center, I have faced many rites of passage without my father, and though I still missed him at every one, I am able to think about those polished stones that Bev gave me long ago and feel comforted. Some days I still feel the jagged edges of the rough rock and it feels like there is a big hole in my soul. The difference now is through Bev's teachings—rather than the shock of such powerful feelings—I am prepared. I can now think of Dad and his amazing smile and feel great joy, fortunate for the time that I had with him. For although I no longer have a father, I know that not many little girls are as lucky as I to be blessed with such pure love and magnetism as my dad exuded every day of his life.

Laurie Richardson

About nine months after my husband was killed in a railroad accident when his train plunged off an open bridge into the Willamette River on a cold foggy night, I was desperate for help. I had read about The Dougy Center in the newspaper. There was one group that met on Wednesday nights and I decided to go with my children. We went for our intake meeting and we felt right at home immediately. The people at The Dougy Center listened, they heard, and they understood what I was talking about.

After that first meeting, I couldn't imagine waiting two weeks to go back again. We did, and we continued to go every other week to support groups for two years. By talking to others in my same situation or in similar situations—each one in varying stages of the grief process—I was able to learn that with help I *would* get through this.

The Dougy Center became my lifeline. Everyone in the outside world wanted to *fix me*, to not see my pain. My pain was there and it was real, and I needed help to understand how to live this new life that was now mine. I made new friends at The Dougy Center, and they understood and supported my family and me. We looked forward to sharing a meal with these people before our group meetings. Everything about this wonderful place welcomed us and the people there did not judge or belittle us because of our pain.

After two years, we somewhat reluctantly decided to leave the center and make room for others. I was not sure that I was really ready to leave because I knew there was a lot more healing that needed to take place. My good friend Judy, from my parent group, and I decided to take the training to become facilitators. The healing continued as we experienced the training and started to facilitate a brand new group for parents. [Laurie and Judy facilitated in an evening group with parents whose child or children had died.] We both felt we would be much better with adults since we were already dealing with grieving children of our own every day.

I later branched out a bit at The Dougy Center and had the opportunity to facilitate the "Littles" with Bev Chappell. I was very excited about this group because I was the parent of a "little guy" who was only three when his father was killed. I continued my healing and I learned so much more from Bev.

During my almost ten years at The Dougy Center I learned so much about myself, my children, and how to deal with my new life. I truly feel that most of the healing took place for me as a facilitator. It was the first time that I ever felt really good at something. I learned how to listen and be present for these parents that were in so much pain. My experience with The Dougy Center changed my life and made me a better person. I treasure my friendships and my experiences more than words can express.

Patrick Richardson

Recently, I spoke with Patrick, 26, who was only three when his father died. Patrick has few memories about his dad's death, or even being with his dad. Much of what he remembers are his older sister's memories. However, Patrick does remember his reaction after his mom told him about his father's death: "I hid in a closet after it happened."

In retrospect, Patrick said, hiding in the closet was just his way of hiding from the reality of what had happened. "I hid inside myself—and I am still doing that a lot," Patrick admitted. "I missed, and still miss, the bonding that a boy has with his father; the camping trips and things dads and their sons do together. One summer Mom, Jenny, and I went on a vacation all summer long. It was fun, but it was really running away from home and all of the sadness there.

"When my dad died, death wasn't a word that I knew," Patrick explained. "I kept asking, 'Where is my daddy?' I was repeatedly told, 'He is dead.' I told them, 'I know that, but when is he going to be over being dead? And when is he coming home?'" Patrick's response to death as a three-year-old is not unusual. For most young children, death is outside of their reality. It is a temporary happening; they believe that soon the one who died will return again.

When we talked about the first couple of years after his dad's death, Patrick said, "The best thing that happened to us was The Dougy Center. It was a safe and warm place to be. People there had the same sadness that we had. We met other kids who had lost their dads and we could talk because we all knew what it was like; we all understood. And being there with Brian [a young facilitator] was special. Brian helped me a lot." Patrick also noted, "And the food was so good."

I had to smile when Patrick talked about the delicious food at The Dougy Center. I remember Patrick's mom saying she was so busy "running" that she absolutely could not cook, and that their car was filled with wrappers and leftover food from more fast food places than anyone could imagine. It is common for grieving families to depend on quick and easy ways to eat since a grieving parent can barely find the motivation to take care of daily needs. This is one of the reasons why communal potluck dinners before the meetings became such an important part of time spent at The Dougy Center. Healthy, nurturing food shared with others always seemed to add to the sense of family and community at the Center.

Patrick was pleased to learn that similar programs are springing up internationally. He acknowledged that grief is a common emotion felt the world over, and he is delighted that other grieving kids are having the same opportunity to heal that he and his family had so many years ago.

Patrick and Jenny Richardson (center) with their support group.

CHAPTER EIGHTEEN

Two Paths to the Dougy Center
Dean Conklin's Story
Clair Zentner's Story

T*here are many paths that lead to The Dougy Center, and each one involves a journey filled with death, grief, healing, and often, offering a helping hand to others. In some cases, people sought out the Center to help others facing the death of a loved one, and along the way realized they had their own unresolved grief. Others come to the Center seeking help, end up taking the volunteer training, and become facilitators themselves.*

The following stories are from two facilitators who arrived at The Dougy Center by different paths. Dean Conklin began volunteering at The Dougy Center two decades ago, planning to help children, yet along the way was helped with his own grief. As of 2007, Dean continues to work with the teen group.

Clair Zentner sought out The Dougy Center with her young children after her husband's death. After finding her own healing, Clair returned to The Dougy Center as a volunteer facilitator, where she continues to work as of 2007.

Dean Conklin's Story

It was April 13, 1945—Friday the 13th—just ten days after my eighth birthday. Ed Conklin, a farmer, rancher, and manager of a Rural Electrification Association (REA), was killed by a jolt from a seventy-two kilovolt electrical cable. I didn't have a daddy any more. For forty years I never spoke about his death, never consciously considered the life-altering significance of this experience.

In 1984, a segment on the television news caught my attention. A nurse, Beverly Chappell, had started a peer support center for children dealing with the death of someone they loved. Months, maybe a year later, I finally mustered the courage to check the place out, take the volunteer training, and become a grief support facilitator.

A cardinal rule of Dougy Center facilitation: Don't confound the group process with our issues. At this point in the game, I hope I won't be fired for a confession. That first year or so in group, a significant part of me became just another eight year old, right there with five, ten, and fifteen year olds—hurting, crying, laughing, hugging a teddy bear, experiencing excruciating, long-buried feelings. I was revisiting the loss of my dad.

Dean Conklin

Thinking back over my years between eight and forty-eight, the "elephant in the parlor" comes to mind. A circle of proper adults perch around the parlor, sipping tea, snacking on hors d'oeuvres, making pleasant conversation: the weather, the kids, the new house, the outrageous price of salmon, that excellent Italian restaurant on Third Avenue. Inexplicably, no one seems to notice, much less comment on, a real live, full-grown Ringling Bros. and Barnum & Bailey elephant, methodically shifting its feet, swinging its trunk, sitting squarely in the center of the room!

Realizing the stunning impact of the death of a loved one—the elephant—on a child's life, Beverly Chappell had the courage, the wisdom, and the vision, to stand, look around the parlor, and say, "Folks, something's amiss here," pointing a finger. "Do you see that elephant? *We must talk about the elephant!*" The rest, as they say, is history.

We all have issues, concerns, and questions around death. There are few clear-cut answers. What we have is our own unique experience, our story. And while that loss will always be with us, becoming who we are, in some ironic sense telling and retelling our story, sharing it with other people, repeating it over and over, is as close as we come to an answer. Until twenty-five years ago, no such place existed for children, or for adults, to tell their story, to explore this life-shaking experience.

Bev's inspiration, her genius, was to create a *safe* place where grieving people have permission to repeat their story, to talk and act out their feelings, the bewilderment, the emptiness, the pain; to express and explore the immensely complex, frightening, overwhelming, violent, impossible-to-describe, "crazy" life triggered by the death of someone we love. Bev found a way to do this work *without* fear of being stigmatized, judged, put down, criticized, advised—without being told not to be angry, not to cry.

So what have I learned after more than two decades at The Dougy Center? Not much really. We are all rookies; we are all experts. We know what to do. We just have to be reminded. It was there in facilitator training, twenty years ago that I had one of my earliest, most significant lessons in grief facilitation: You are not here to "fix" people. How many times did I hear it? How many times have I wanted to fix someone—another confession—or how many times have I *tried* to "fix' em?" But I can't. Fortunately, I don't have to because they are *not broke*! Grief is not something gone wrong, a problem to be solved. Grief is our mind/body/spirit's means of incorporating loss into life, a healing that never really ends.

Over the sixty years since my dad died, I revisit and deal with that fact on a continuing basis. Until twenty years ago virtually all of those dealings, such as they were, were chaotic and unconscious. At The Dougy Center I finally found the safety and permission necessary to face and finally, methodically—at least somewhat more methodically—come to grips with the most significant, the most defining event of my life.

Clair Zentner's Story

I first heard about The Dougy Center from a friend after my husband, Jeff, died of a cocaine overdose on February 9, 1988. It had been nightmarish ever since his first overdose and hospitalization in April 1987, when I first learned of his dependency on drugs. At that time, we were given information for drug treatment programs and we learned all about dysfunctional family systems. Jeff had always been the one in control and I believed he would be okay. However, Jeff was in and out of programs—inpatient and outpatient—for the next ten months. He couldn't stay clean.

Prior to my husband's death, life had become stressful and chaotic for our family; lies to his boss after not showing up for work, twelve-step meetings, trying to be strong for our two children and myself, and dealing with Jeff's depression. The longest he remained clean was five weeks.

Clair Zentner

On the home front, I was trying to take care of things financially, but we just didn't have the money to cover all of our bills. Drug abuse is very expensive. I had contacted Consumer Credit Counseling, but they said they couldn't help us. I was in the process of contacting all of our creditors to make payment arrangements, but it seemed that bankruptcy was looming in our future. I kept thinking that everything could be all right, but Jeff would have to stay clean and go back to work.

After a second overdose, my husband went through a twenty-one day treatment program. Jeff left his third rehab on Saturday, February 6, 1988. When I came home that day, I learned that Jeff had been reading to our son, David, which was rare but really nice. Jeff told David they would play basketball the next afternoon. I don't think he had ever done that. Things were looking up and our little seven-year-old was very happy. Then my husband was off to his twelve-step meeting to get together with his other recovering friends. I was pretty numb, but kissed Jeff goodbye. That was the last time we ever saw him.

Jeff didn't come home that night and I couldn't sleep much. I considered going out to look for him; but where? I was always trying to fix things. Now, I was learning to accept things I couldn't control. I thought to myself, *If he ran off the road into a ditch, the police will find him and call.* I felt confident Jeff would come home the next day even though I didn't hear from him all day. Still, I felt he would be home when I got there.

That day at my job with the phone company, I got a phone call that didn't concern me too much. A man was asking to speak to my supervisor and I immediately thought, *Perhaps I have done something wrong.* As I was getting ready to leave work I decided to put on some make-up, which I didn't do very often. I was looking forward to seeing my husband and wanted to look nice. As I was putting on make-up, my best friend came into the rest room and told me my supervisor was looking for me. As soon as I saw the expression on my supervisor's face, I knew something was very wrong. He wanted to talk to me, but somewhere private, so we started upstairs to his manager's office. As we were going up the stairs, I stopped in mid-step, turned, looked at him, and said, "He's dead, isn't he?" Some moments just stand still in time for a lifetime.

It so happened I had an Aftercare meeting. This program worked hand-in-hand with my husband's drug rehab treatment program. It was where the spouses met for support while their partners participated in the rehabilitation program.

My group was meeting that afternoon, which was a relief. I had somewhere to go where people would understand what I was facing. When I walked in and was so upset, the facilitator knew what had happened. She had not seen Jeff recovering and wasn't surprised. Later, I learned that my husband had gone to a couple twelve-step meetings that last night, and friends said he even spoke and was upbeat. But at midnight, Jeff went to an ATM machine and withdrew $100.

The next day a maid found his body in a motel room. He had been very depressed and medication didn't seem to help. Jeff always had to be in control and being hooked on drugs was horrible for him. I am sure he had a tremendous amount of guilt and shame, and a sense that we were all paying for his actions. No doubt my husband felt he could never break the cycle of drug use, and the addiction finally broke him. That is why I have believed it was a suicide, not accidental.

My next task was to go home and tell our two young children—Judi, ten, and David, seven. My brother-in-law had gone to the coroner's office and identified his brother's body. (It was the coroner's office that had called me looking for my supervisor.) My brother-in-law and his wife were with me when my children came home. I didn't know what else to say to them but the truth. I was in shock. I kept thinking, *How are we supposed to manage?* We had plans for our lives. He wasn't supposed to die. How would I raise two children? I had been raised in a family where the husband ruled. My marriage worked the same way. I didn't have a lot of self-confidence and here I was, thrown from the frying pan into the fire. I stood there for a moment, looking at our children, and then knew I had to go on. I had to take care of the three of us.

I had to tell others what had happened and that was hard. No one in our nice neighborhood in the suburbs knew he was in such trouble. A friend who watched Judi and David told me about The Dougy Center. I called right away. I had to do something.

When I first called The Dougy Center there was a waiting list, but they had the "Monthly Meeting" for people. When we went, it was my first experience in a group like that. I had no idea so many people died and so many people were grieving just like me and my children. There were a myriad of types of deaths, most of them private, but some that made the newspaper. Suddenly, I was in a club. We were a club of grievers trying to pick up the pieces and carry on. But we were all still in shock and numb.

The Dougy Center was growing and the staff had decided to start two new groups: "Healing from Suicide," and "Healing from Violent Death and Murder." My family didn't have to wait long. We were one of the first families in the "Healing from Suicide" group.

From the beginning, when we had our first intake appointment with Izetta Smith, I felt safe at The Dougy Center. That feeling has never left. They were there for the children and me—and they knew we would be all right. We attended our groups at the Center and I could feel the lightness returning in my children each time we left group meetings. My son was very active. He talked and formed a bond with the facilitators. My daughter never wanted to talk much about her experience at The Dougy Center. She did her grief work in a different manner. Judi was quiet in the meetings and at home, but she did grieve in her own way and in her own time. I always worried about my children, and I would frequently ask facilitators how they were doing. The facilitators would only smile and say, "Your children are doing their work." That meant all was well.

We attended our groups for more than two years. My daughter was ready to make a closure first, and then my son, who at first thought he would continue until he was sixteen when he would be able to drive himself to group. After a tragedy, it is hard to fathom that things will get better and it will be okay to move on.

In 1991, ABC's program, "20/20," did a segment on The Dougy Center. The reporter, John Stossel, interviewed David, who was ten years old at the time, for the segment. In the news story, Stossel told the television audience that David's father had died of a cocaine overdose. He asked David if, or how, The Dougy Center had helped him. David answered, "I can't talk to my friends about it 'cause everyone else has parents. I have friends, but I don't really trust them. If I talked to them, it would be around school in ten minutes, and I don't want that."

Then Stossel asked, "Why is it so bad if other people know? It's not as if you did something wrong." David replied, "It's sort of hard. It is awkward, 'cause everyone else has parents and you are missing someone."

At one point in the interview, Stossel asked, "Do you ever feel like your father is coming back?" David replied, "I felt like my father was in the walls and he just had a little hole so he could get out, and like, during the night when I was asleep. He wouldn't talk to me. He just stood there and we sorta' looked at each other. I asked him, 'You're alive?' I thought he would come out some day." Then David added, "That day he died, my dad was going to play basketball with me and it's like around 5 o'clock and he didn't show up. Then that night my mom told me—and it's like if I had just told him like to do this at this time—pick me up after school ...." David's voice trailed off. Then Stossel asked, "You could have saved him?" David answered, "Maybe."

Several years after we completed at The Dougy Center, I had a realization that led me back to the Center as a volunteer. After September 11, 2001, watching the news coverage and the focus on the families and children in New York, it finally hit me that there were families right here in Oregon going through crises, too. I remembered how traumatized I was by my husband's death and decided it was time to be there for other families. Lives were shattered, and I learned, firsthand, there is a proven way to help where it is really needed.

Shortly after the national tragedy of 9/11, I took a facilitator training at The Dougy Center. After my training, I joined one of the "Healing from a Sudden Death" groups in November 2001. At first, I was so uncomfortable, thinking I didn't know how to do this. As time went on, I learned that our job as facilitators is to be present for the families and they will do the work they need to do. It has been more than four years now, and I feel I have helped to make a difference for the families. I have been at the Center long enough to see families arrive in tears and leave with smiles. It is a privilege to meet these courageous children—and also adults who are doing what is necessary for their children, as I did for mine. I will be forever grateful for what The Dougy Center has done for us, and the experience of being there for others.

CHAPTER NINETEEN

Volunteer Facilitators

Since the beginning, The Dougy Center's lifeline has been its volunteers. Without a dedicated group of individuals sharing the vision of The Dougy Center, this special place for grieving children and their families never would have taken off and flourished. This still holds true today, twenty-five years after our first support group. There is no sufficient amount of praise I can give these volunteer facilitators. From the beginning, they were the key to making a successful grief support program for children and their families.

During the first couple of years when we were trying to get the word out to the public about The Dougy Center, we got a lot of help from our local television station, KOIN-TV. This television station ran numerous public service announcements on our behalf, broadcasting our need for volunteers. These public service announcements brought volunteers to work as facilitators at The Dougy Center as well as reaching families looking for help while coping with death and grief. KOIN-TV also sponsored several fund-raising events for the Center, which helped tremendously.

We call individuals who help in support groups "facilitators," not "counselors." Since the inception of the Center, we agreed not to do counseling or therapy in the support groups. We trained facilitators to be a part of the families' healing process, and to help the children and their parents share their experiences. Our idea of a facilitator was someone who listened well, and only stepped in when the conversation and communication came to a standstill. In the early years of The Dougy Center, we held trainings every six months if we had at least twelve people who wanted to become facilitators. Within three to four years we had a waiting list of people who wished to take the training and get involved with the program. Many of these people heard about The Dougy Center from the public service announcements.

During the first session of each facilitator training, we sat in a circle and asked each person to share what brought him or her to the training and why they were interested in working with grieving children and/or adults. The responses were eye opening. Almost every one of the volunteers was dealing with unresolved grief in his or her life. It might have been a spouse who died, a parent who died when they were younger, or even more recently, the death of a child, a sibling, or a close friend. We, as staff, learned as much about grief while doing the facilitator trainings as we did working with the children and parents in the groups. To this day, these trainings continue to be golden opportunities for the staff to deal with their unresolved grief as well as train group facilitators.

The Challenges and Gifts for Facilitators

When the children and teens' groups began, we used the Native American tradition of the "talking stick" as a way to help the children listen to one another. At the beginning of the group, one of the facilitators would hand a child the talking stick, a crystal-and-feather adorned dowel. This signified that the person holding the talking stick had

BEVERLY CHAPPELL

Facilitators for the first "Healing from Suicide" group, now called "Healing from a Suicide Death." Bev was also a facilitator, but was taking the photo.

the group's attention and could talk while the others listened. The children passed the talking stick around the circle and each person had an opportunity to say what was going on in his or her life; what had been extreme-

Participants and facilitators in the "Sons & Daughters II" group.

ly difficult, and in which areas healing may have taken place. The children also understood that if a person was not ready to talk, he or she could pass on taking a turn, and the talking stick would be passed to the next person. If the person who passed up a turn changed his or her mind later, the talking stick was passed back so the child could have the opportunity to speak.

Depending on the group, the opening circle could take three minutes if the kids wanted to move on to an activity, or the opening circle could take an hour and a half for everyone to check in. It always depended on what was needed at any given moment. This is still the case at the Center.

The group facilitators helped to keep the conversations going, encouraging those who had not spoken, but they never pushed if someone did not want to participate. At times, a facilitator needed to step in and calm things down, especially if siblings experienced the death of a family member in different ways and started arguing about what had "really happened." In time, we learned that each person may have experienced the same death in a completely different way, depending on his or her relationship with, or memories of, the deceased loved one.

Most of the facilitators loved what they were doing and stayed in their groups for many years. Some of the people who took the training in the early days of The Dougy Center are still facilitating groups more than twenty years later. When asked why they have stayed so long, they all assure me, "We get far more from what we are doing than from what we give." I know this is true; I was a facilitator for many years, too!

As previously mentioned, most of these wonderful people came to this program burdened by their own grief experiences. They not only were the perfect ones to help others who were grieving, but in a large sense were able to assuage a great amount of their own grief while helping others. When people put themselves in such a deep and painful situation such as working with grieving children or adults, one of two things is bound to happen: The volunteers either begin to heal themselves or they have to leave the program because it is too intense a situation for them. Very few have left.

The Volunteers' Voices

In the course of writing this book, I asked many different people involved with the Center to share their memories. In particular, I wanted to hear from the volunteers who have been the Center's lifeline down through the years. I asked a number of volunteers to write a note telling me why they came to The Dougy Center; what they did there; and what they received from their time in a support group. I would like to share the words of some of those who responded.

BRIAN JACKSON was one of the first volunteers to work with me as a facilitator when we were meeting in our home. Brian's mother had died of cancer when he was sixteen, and my family and I were close to Brian as he stayed close to his mother during her final illness and death. (See Chapter One.) After college, I asked Brian if he would work with the

Brian Jackson working on the Warner Pacific House.

fledgling Dougy Center as a facilitator. I thought he would be excellent because he understood death and grief, and he was still a young adult and could relate to how the children in the support group felt. It was mid-1983, and although Brian was reticent at first, he had a change of heart. Recalling that time in his life, Brian wrote:

> I remember as if it had happened an hour ago. I had the thought that I needed to do something for someone else; something that required me not to be so caught up in my own stuff of the moment.

I thought of Bev and what she was doing with kids who had suffered a loss. One day as I started across the room to pick up the telephone and call Bev, the phone rang. It was Bev calling again to see if by now I might have reconsidered volunteering. Without hesitation I said, "Yes." Then I asked her to explain again what she was doing. I was still unclear about what happened at The Dougy Center, but I didn't care. I just knew in my gut that I wanted to be part of it.

As I look back, I know my experience of having a parent die during my childhood brought me to The Dougy Center for several reasons. This gave me the opportunity to help kids who had their own losses. Working as a facilitator also gave me the opportunity to do some more processing around my own mother's death. It also gave me a place to be while I underwent new losses in my life. I no doubt learned more from the kids and my co-facilitators than they learned from me, but that is what it was about. Being there for one another; learning from one another. We are each other's teachers."

BETTY ASHFORD became a facilitator within the first year of The Dougy Center's operation, and some twenty-five years later continues to keep closely in touch with the happenings at the Center. She told me that the roots of her Dougy Center experience began with meeting Gerald Jampolsky, who founded The Center for Attitudinal Healing in Tiburon, California. Betty was so impressed with Jampolsky's work that she called the Tiburon center to learn more about it. Betty found out that the center offered support for children with catastrophic illnesses, and the center's philosophy was inspired by *A Course in Miracles*, which deals with universal spiritual themes. In a nutshell, *A Course in Miracles* teaches that forgiveness is the road to inner peace.

Lynn Knope (left), Allan Chappell and Betty Ashford

It wasn't long after meeting Jampolsky that Betty heard about The Dougy Center. At that time, it was under consideration whether or not to include ideas from *A Course in Miracle*s as part of the curriculum at The Dougy Center. However, from the beginning we had decided that The Dougy Center would be nonsecular, and although many of us personally agreed with some of the course's philosophy, we decided not to formally include it in the Center's philosophy.

When Betty learned that three or four people from The Dougy Center had visited The Center for Attitudinal Healing to learn about its approach to working with children, she decided to inquire further. "I found that The Dougy Center was patterned in many ways after The Center for Attitudinal Healing, but focusing on grieving children who had lost a parent, or a sibling," explained Betty. "Since I had lost my mother to cancer and my husband to a fatal accident not long before learning about The Dougy Center, I was drawn to the Center."

At the time, Betty had recently received a Master's degree in Counseling Psychology and felt she might have skills that would be needed. The core group developing The Dougy Center program in its early days included Bev Fulk, Izetta Smith, Jim Hussey and me. We all welcomed Betty as a volunteer. In fact, we quickly found Betty's perspective valuable and used her as a sounding board when we found ourselves going in opposite directions in our plans for The Dougy Center.

Betty began as a facilitator in the first parent group, and later we asked her to be on the staff part-time as a coordinator, visiting all the groups as an experienced helper or, as she described it, "a nanny." "Each group often began with a time of meditation and/or music," recalled Betty. "The participants quickly became a substitute family for each other. The staff was a small, talented, dedicated group of men and women, but the heart of The Dougy Center was the many volunteers. They created a loving nest for parents and children to be nurtured. They shared their grief as well as their healing with each other and made life-long friends. For me, The Dougy Center was a spiritually-founded, life-changing experience."

LYNN KNOPE was another early facilitator who eventually became a staff member and a group coordinator. She loved her work at The Dougy Center, and took graduate classes in psychology during that time. No longer at The Dougy Center, Lynn is now a licensed psychologist with her own practice working with children, adults, and families. The following are some of her recollections of the early years at The Dougy Center and what she describes as a very unique experience.

> When I think about what impacted me the most at The Dougy Center, two things come to mind. First of all, I was drawn to the nature of the work in all its intensity, rawness, and strength. The pain that children experience when there is a death in the family is so big that it defies being described.
>
> Perhaps it feels as though their world has been turned upside down, shaken up, and twisted. Then they are dumped out in a deep, dark, hole from which there is no escape. And yet, the human spirit struggles to crawl out of this hole, inch by inch. The human spirit continues on life's path while dragging this tremendous burden, day after day, seeking the light it knows is there, but is so dim in the distance. Eventually, the light begins to brighten, and the load begins to feel less heavy. The children grow stronger, until they are ready to stand with their feet planted once again, and face the world, and invest in new relationships. This time they see the world through different eyes, with hearts that hold more compassion, for themselves and others.
>
> The second aspect that was so remarkable was the feminist perspective that created the underpinnings of the organizational structure at The Dougy Center. The experience of all who participated was sought, and most of all from the children, as they were our teachers. In addition, the gifts from all were cherished; the staff, the volunteers, and the families and their children.
>
> The holding environment that was created and that was congruent throughout the organization was remarkable: the board holding the director, the director holding the clinical supervisor, the supervisor holding the line staff, the line staff holding the volunteers, the volunteers holding the families. It was the most congruent professional work experience I have had to date. My memories from my days at The Dougy Center are ones that I hold close to my heart. The philosophy, the beliefs, the values, created the underpinnings of my current work with children, families, and adults.

BARBARA DOOLEY BUECHLE was one of the early volunteers at The Dougy Center. She facilitated the children's group with me in "Sons and

Daughters I." Barbara was there several years until she married, and her life went in a different direction. Barbara told me that at first, she didn't really know why she came to The Dougy Center. She told herself it was because she wanted to "work with children who were dying—to comfort, play, and hug these special children." Looking back, Barbara laughed as she explained what happened.

Facilitators Connie Lloyd (right) and Barbara Dooley Buechle with a participant

When I visited The Dougy Center, I soon discovered that there were no dying children, just a house at the Warner Pacific complex that needed some tender loving care. Dedicated volunteers were scrubbing, scraping, and painting the old house, so I did, too. Bev and Al showed me what to do; they also listened to my stories and told me theirs. [Barbara had recently moved to Oregon and needed some companionship.] Little by little the house took shape and in the process I learned about The Dougy Center.

Through the years and with conversations with Izetta, Lucy, Laurie, and many others, and with help from the trainings, I discovered I was really at The Dougy Center for *me* because I was grieving. I had come to The Dougy Center to be with people who could comfort, hug, and love me. As I learned more about The Dougy Center, I gradually moved from the volunteer status to being a staff member. Through the years I treasured the moments I could sit with my fellow Dougy Center staff and share our thoughts. I found that their love, friendship, guidance, and words of wisdom helped me through the deaths of my sister and my mother.

In hindsight, Barbara told me she feels the education, information, stories, friendships, love, and growth at The Dougy Center became her facilitation for daily living. A few years ago when Barbara's mother-in-law was dying, her work and experiences at The Dougy Center helped her be an active participant in her mother-in-law's death. She was also able to be present for her family—as well as for herself.

ERIC GRISWOLD was among the first facilitators at The Dougy Center, and in the early years offered his talents as a photographer. Some of his wonderful photographs grace this book. Eric shared some of his memories of his time at the Center:

Eric Griswold

> I met Bev Chappell and came to The Dougy Center around 1985. I had lost a child from SIDS in the late 1960s and was still working through my grief around that loss. Facilitating at The Dougy Center gave me an opportunity to be around children and to keep loss and grief in my awareness so I could understand and move through it better myself.
>
> What struck me and moved me at the time, and has stayed with me ever since, is how everyone at The Dougy Center participated in bringing their own offering of unconditional love into the mix. This was not just an occasional experience; the commitment to unconditional love was woven into every decision and every facet of The Dougy Center. Although I have not experienced the same level of synergy since, I carry with me from those years of facilitating the knowledge that it is real and it is possible. I continue to call it a safe warm nest. What a gift!

BARBIE RICE began volunteering at The Dougy Center in 1992 and to this day continues working on many levels at the Center. Barbie described the path that led her to The Dougy Center:

Barbie Rice

> Fifteen years ago I was working with the dying in the patient wing of a hospice called Hopewell House. While I was doing my work there, I would see patients die, and I always wondered and worried about the little children. I often wondered, *What would happen to them? How would they handle their grief and how would they heal?* Then I learned about a magical place called The Dougy Center. I was drawn to learn about this Center and immediately wanted to become a part of it.
>
> Although I chose to work at The Dougy Center because of my interest and concern for grieving children, I have received so much

more than I have given. It is an amazing privilege to have a tiny part in helping a child heal from pain and grief. I have learned the art of being "present" and of "listening" as well as compassion and hope. My work with children at The Dougy Center has given me a deeper appreciation of life and all I am blessed with. These brave children continue to be my teachers and I remain in awe of their courage. The Dougy Center truly is a safe place where "kids take care of kids."

Along with family, friends, and more hours than I care to admit in psychotherapy, The Dougy Center remains a crucial focus of my world. I would even say, in a sense, The Dougy Center helped save my life. At this time in 2007, I am a facilitator in the "Healing from a Suicide Death" group, a member of the Advisory Board, and during my fifteen years at the Center, I have served as a facilitator in children and teen groups.

Chris McClave

CHRIS McCLAVE first learned about The Dougy Center in April 1987, and the following year began volunteering. She has been an integral part of the Center ever since. Chris served as Chair of the board of directors during some extremely crucial years. Her years of commitment have been inspired by personal loss as well as a passion for the vision of The Dougy Center.

Today, Chris facilitates children's groups every Thursday afternoon alternating between the "Healing from a Suicide Death" group one week and the "Healing from Violent Death/Homicide" group the next. She also gives orientations to people who come to The Dougy Center to seek help with their grief, and helps them decide which group will work best for them. Chris wrote the following recollections of her time at The Dougy Center:

I was introduced to Bev Chappell by a friend of mine who at that time was on the board of directors for The Dougy Center. Within fifteen minutes of hearing Bev's passion for the center, I was hooked. The timing was not the best for me, in one sense, because May of 1986 brought tragedy and chaos into my life. My seventeen-year-old daughter was killed in a mountain-climbing accident on Mt. Hood. This event both stopped my life—and started me down a path through the world of grief, about which I knew very little. What I did know after meeting with Bev was that I needed more time to take care of myself before I could be a support to other grieving adults and children. In January 1988, I began my journey with Bev and her beloved Dougy Center.

Over the years, The Dougy Center has given me more gifts than I could ever have imagined would come my way. I joined the board of directors and twelve years later finally realized my personal goal of being able to leave the board with the organization financially stable and a young and energetic group of board members who could take the organization forward. This was hard, challenging work and I don't have a single regret. The sleepless nights of wondering how in the world we would survive financially, how I would rise to the occasion as Board Chair over a six year period and two Executive Directors, and serve the organization and the community with honesty, integrity, and grace are now a gentle memory.

The opportunity to be part of a grass roots organization with an annual budget of approximately $35,000 to becoming the national and international organization it is today is something for which I will be eternally grateful. I was pushed and challenged to stretch my mind and soul. I went from "sure, I would be happy to be a board member, but don't ask me to raise any money" to learning that it is not really "fund-raising" but "friend-raising" that builds the ever so critical financial footing necessary to operate. I had never been a board member before and when asked to be the chair, I sought some advice from a friend about how to operate. He said, "There are three things you need to know; delegate… delegate… delegate." Believe me, I did that very well.

If you have never sat with a grieving family you have missed a very profound moment. It is possible to witness great courage, great pain, great joy, great sadness all mixed together within a few minutes of time. That is what grief has the capacity to produce in a person. My work with the children and adults at the center has been, and continues to this day, to be my earning the equivalent of a Ph.D. in perhaps, "Understanding the Human Condition and Bearing Witness to the Human Spirit."

Thursday afternoons have been my time for eighteen years to be with families at the center. There has never been a Thursday that I haven't walked away from the group time, facilitating with either the children or the adults, that I have not felt that I have received a gift and gained new knowledge about life and death.

It would be foolish of me to say that my work at the center has not been a part of my healing from the death of my daughter. Quite the opposite. When I see children, listen to their stories of loss, walk with them on their journey, it feeds my soul. I believe courage is born of pain. Grief can cause great pain, but when shared in a safe place with others, the jagged edges of grief and tragedy become rounded. The children at the center bring tremendous courage with them and they work to round out the jagged edges of their grief. Their courage is contagious and I have caught it. It has been a tremendous privilege and an honor to have been a part of this powerful process and it is my hope that I will be able to continue for many years to come."

LORETTA CUKALE has been a facilitator for twenty years, working with teens and young adults, and still draws deep satisfaction from the work. Her son, Tony, and his best friend, Kelly, were killed in an auto accident in 1981. They were both sixteen years old. "This loss caused me to start an inward spiritual journey," explained Cukale. "It was the most transformational event of my life. This also began my journey

Loretta Cukale

toward The Dougy Center. In the following years, my difficult marriage became more challenging and through the separation and subsequent divorce, I began to challenge my religious and personal beliefs. Through my searching and readings I was introduced to the writings of Gerald Jampolsky and the concept of attitudinal healing. The Dougy Center was originally focused in that direction and that was all I needed to hear, so I signed up."

Loretta began her facilitator's training at The Dougy Center in January 1987. Even though she felt she had gone through her grieving over the death of her son, the training helped her look at some deeper layers of grief around her son as well as the death of her mother and father. Loretta also liked that the principles on which the Center was founded complemented her spiritual beliefs. "It was refreshing to be able to share my feelings without any judgment from others who also shared losses," Loretta explained, "and to be with others who also had a desire to volunteer with those who were grieving." She recalled the facilitator training as intense for her—nothing like she had imagined it would be.

Through the training Loretta learned to be an active listener, which she explained, has helped her in all areas of her life. Loretta emphasized that training to be a facilitator really prepared her to trust that each individual has within him or herself the capacity to heal if given an opportunity to be heard in an unconditional way, without judgment, and in a safe environment. Her mantra became, and still is, *trust the process.* When Loretta completed her training in March 1987, a teen group had just been formed. "Of course, that was the group I wanted to be with," recalled Loretta. "Remembering my desire to volunteer with teens in grief, this was the answer to that desire and prayer."

Loretta still feels it is a privilege to volunteer in this capacity. She trusts that she does not have to do anything but be present and listen without judgment. "I am in constant awe of the teens for their courage, strength, wisdom, and capacity to be real, and to share their feelings," Loretta explained. "I am honored by the trust that they place in us. I have learned so much from them. I am forever grateful to the founder, Bev Chappell, for her vision for the Center. And for the staff, past and present, who continue to support all of the facilitators in their efforts."

BEVERLY CHAPPELL

On-call Teddy bears waiting for children.

Loretta also made a special note to express her gratitude for her fellow facilitators with whom she shares a common bond, and for the special friendships she has developed over the years. But the main reason she continues to volunteer is the healing that she sees in the participants, and to witness their transformations. Loretta feels that it is most rewarding to see their pain progress to renewal and says, "Even though The Dougy Center has gone through many changes over the past years, the program and the process continue to be the same—and it works."

CHAPTER TWENTY

The Dougy Center Today

The Dougy Center began in 1982 with four children and one support group. Since that simple beginning twenty-five years ago, it has grown to serve more than 20,000 children, teens, young adults, and families. The Center has received national and international acclaim for its pioneering support model for helping children cope with the death of a family member. Today, The Dougy Center serves more than 350 children and their 200 adult family members each month.

As of 2007, Donna Schuurman, Ed.D., continues to serve as the Center's Executive Director. Donna has emboldened the vision of The Dougy Center along with many dedicated and loyal volunteers and staff. She has steered the Center to an international role as a source of information and resources for grieving children and their families. Over the years, Donna has written books, manuals, and articles on grief under the auspices of The Dougy Center, such as *When Death Impacts Your School* or *35 Ways to Help a Grieving Child*. Most recently, she authored, *Never the Same: Coming to Terms with the Death of a Parent* (St. Martin's Press, 2004). These publications have been tremendously helpful to thousands of individuals, groups, and organizations dealing with grieving children.

While preparing this overview of The Dougy Center today, I asked Donna to share some thoughts on her role as executive director for the past sixteen years. Donna wrote:

> Serving as The Dougy Center's Executive Director since 1991, along with four years prior to that as a volunteer facilitator, has been a profoundly rewarding journey. The children, teens, young adults, and their adult family members come to the Center after unimaginable

losses, vulnerable, often afraid, and searching. To be trusted with the soul's story of another human being is a gift many do not get to experience in their work lives, and I feel privileged indeed.

Additionally, I have had the privilege to work with amazing staff and dedicated volunteers who have been inspirations and who have put up admirably with my management learning curve over the years.

There's no way to include everyone who has made The Dougy Center what it is today, but I particularly want to recognize three volunteers. Christine McClave, a long-time volunteer and previous Chair of The Dougy Center's Board of Directors, stepped in for several months in 1990/1991 as Interim Executive Director between my predecessor's departure and my hire in March 1991. Chris showed up, took a big risk in assuming a role she felt unprepared for, and kept things together during a time things could easily have fallen apart. Later, she spearheaded board and community fund-raising efforts with a fervor any nonprofit executive would envy, even though she first joined the board saying she'd do anything but fund raise!

Michael Hubbard, another volunteer who owns the dubious distinction of most recurring chairmanships of the board of directors, stepped in at another one of those seminal times to lead by example. He also donated shares of stock, which ultimately provided financial breathing room to a struggling organization just making payroll each month.

And finally, another long-time volunteer facilitator, Gwyneth Gamble Booth, founded our advisory board over fifteen years ago, advocating in every venue of her significant community involvement for the Center's mission and needs.

I owe each of them a tremendous debt of thanks, and without their leadership and perseverance, I do not believe The Dougy Center would be in existence today.

Current Support Groups and Outreach

The breadth and depth of the grief support groups at The Dougy Center have grown far beyond what we could have imagined in the early days. I asked Donna to describe the variety of support groups as of 2007. The following is her overview of the Center's outreach:

The Dougy Center now has twenty-four open-ended children's and teens' peer support groups that meet every other week and are divided by age and mode of death, as well as who died. These groups include "Littles" for three-to-five-year-olds who have had a parent die. Groups for six-to-twelve-year-olds include "Sons & Daughters" for those who had a parent die; "Sibs" groups for those who had a sibling die; "Healing from a Suicide Death;" "Healing from a Violent Death;" and groups for sudden/unexpected death, as well as deaths from illness or disease. Teen peer groups are for thirteen-to-eighteen-year-olds who have experienced the death of a family member or friend.

In September 2003, a new "Young Adults Group" at The Dougy Center began to serve nineteen-to-thirty-year-olds. This group is for young adults who have experienced the death of someone in their lives in their childhood, adolescent years, or recently. What appears to be most important, and most bonding with this group is that they share similar life challenges such as leaving home, making decisions about future schooling, work, marriage, and children, and all of the attendant pressures and uncertainties that go with being a young adult. For some young adults, the impact of a parent or sibling's death in childhood is coming to the forefront in new ways as adults. Others in the group have experienced the recent loss of a parent, sibling, friend or partner.

Young adults seem to be a "gap age" with limited services that address their specific time in adulthood. They're not comfortable in widow/widower groups if they have had a husband or wife die since most of those groups are filled with people in later life stages. People in the Center's "Young Adults Group" have the opportunity to share with their peers, regardless of when a significant death occurred in their lives. This common thread helps them to normalize their experience, to know when to seek additional help if needed, and to have others who understand.

At first, The Dougy Center staff assumed a concurrent "parent" group would not be needed for the "Young Adults Group." We thought they would not be interested in having their parent or parents involved at the same level as Dougy Center participants under eighteen. However, we soon learned the participants in the "Young Adults Group" asked for a similar support group—a group they could invite a friend, spouse, or partner to, in order to have that much-needed support.

Several of the young adults had attended Dougy Center groups when they were younger, and the new challenges they face in early adulthood have revived or revealed different aspects of the long-term impact of their losses. As we like to say at The Dougy Center, "Grief doesn't end. It shifts form, ebbs and flows, and varies in intensity and form, but we are forever changed by the death of someone important in our lives."

In addition to the support groups, The Dougy Center also offers a variety of workshops and trainings for organizations and individuals working with grieving children in hospitals, schools, hospices, youth service organizations and mental health agencies. All of the off-site trainings are "custom-developed" to the needs of the training site, and may be focused on how to start a local program for grieving children, or any range of specialized topics. For example, programs may include "How Schools/Communities Best Respond to a Suicide Death"; "Helping Teens Cope with Death"; or "Community Response to Violent Death."

A good example of the type of outreach and intervention Dougy Center staff offer took place in 1998 after a school shooting in Oregon. Donna described this dramatic intervention in The Dougy Center's newsletter:

> Because of the type of work we do at The Dougy Center, there's never down time; death doesn't take a vacation.... We respond to hundreds of calls monthly from around the country for advice and referrals, conducted trainings, and provided interventions in the community following deaths.
>
> One of those interventions was in Springfield, Oregon following the tragic shootings at Thurston High School. As fate would have it, Joan Schweizer Hoff, the Associate Director of The Dougy Center, was conducting a training for Crime Victim Advocates from all over Oregon at their 15th Annual Conference the morning of May 21, 1998. Her topic? "The Impact of Violent Death on Children."
>
> Joan's presentation was interrupted by someone bursting in to share the news about the shootings at Thurston High School. Joan was also contacted by Washington, D.C.-based NOVA, the National Organization for Victim Assistance, to serve on their 15-member

team commissioned by Attorney General Janet Reno and President
Clinton. Over the next week, Joan participated with the team and
other professionals who rushed to Springfield to assist in debriefing
teens who witnessed the shooting; listening to and comforting other
students; and developing and implementing a coherent plan amidst
a chaotic scene.

The Dougy Center staff responded similarly with the Oklahoma
City bombing on April 19, 1995. A couple of staff members traveled
to Oklahoma City after the bombing to give trainings for dealing with
death and grief. After the tragedy of September 11, 2001, Donna
was involved with trainings in New York City. The Center's outreach
locally, nationally, and internationally continues to grow.

Within Oregon, The Dougy Center opened a satellite program in
2005 located in Canby, just south of Portland. The expansion location
was made possible through the generosity of Warren and Bernice
Bean, who started the Walker L. Bean Foundation in memory of their
fifteen-year-old son, Walker, who died of suicide. The Foundation
bought a house and loans it to The Dougy Center as a meeting place
for grief support groups. Willamette Falls Hospital and The Dougy
Center have partnered to serve families in the area for whom a longer
drive to Portland may be impossible.

Most recently, The Dougy Center added bilingual grief support
groups at the center as well as at off-site locations in Oregon. The
bilingual coordinator at The Dougy Center, Ruben Garcia, recruits
and trains bilingual volunteers, and networks with organizations and
professionals within Latino communities in Oregon. The Dougy
Center also started publishing its materials in Spanish for more effective outreach.

International Outreach

Every year The Dougy Center hosts its International Summer
Institute for people interested in starting a grieving center for children
and teens. An important part of this training session is hands-on
experience for running peer support groups for children, teens, young
adults, and parents. The Summer Institute offers in-depth information
and advice on administration, fund-raising, marketing, and development

of a board of directors.

Joan Schweizer Hoff, the current Director of Program Services at The Dougy Center, has been with the Center since 1992. She is an integral part of the Center's outreach, both nationally and internationally. Joan leads the training sessions at The Dougy Center, often developing individual sessions to meet the needs of those attending. In addition to the Summer Institute, Joan, Donna, and other staff members travel to communities worldwide to help train volunteers and staff. Explaining The Dougy Center's outreach, Joan writes:

> The International Summer Institute has been held yearly since 1987. In those 20 years we have trained more than 400 people from the United States and internationally in The Dougy Center model. Many of those trained have gone back to their homes and started centers using the information they have learned.
>
> There are currently 165 centers that have been started using our model in 47 states and 9 countries providing grief groups for children, teens, and their families. In addition to the centers in the United States, we have trained people from Australia, New Zealand, England, Germany, Ireland, Switzerland, Israel, Japan, Mexico, Jamaica, Canada, Uganda, and the Congo.

Many groups have adapted, changed or stretched The Dougy Center's model to include, for example, services to children before a death; individual and/or group counseling; or therapy groups, among other services. We know that there are many different ways to help grieving children, teens, young adults and their families, and The Dougy Center model is just one way. Donna notes:

> While The Dougy Center staff provides training in our program, which operates with a specific model, this is not a franchise and we do not expect other people to follow in our exact footsteps.
>
> For instance, The Dougy Center is open-ended, which means families participate for the length of time they wish to. We also have open groups in which people are entering and leaving rather than maintaining a specific group that has the same people in it for a specified time. The Dougy Center groups are non-curriculum-driven, although we provide a structure for the groups with the main focus on re-empowering a sense of control by "following" rather than

"leading" the group. Most importantly, The Dougy Center offers peer support—not therapy. We encourage people to adapt our model to meet their own community needs.

Institute participants leave these Dougy Center training sessions with the hope that they, too, will someday have a "home" like The Dougy Center to help hurting children. For many of them, the hope becomes reality as they use their new knowledge to start programs, both small and large.

Grieving Centers from Africa to Asia and Beyond

The International Summer Institute has drawn people from Africa, Asia, Europe, the Middle East, and North America. The attendees come from a variety of backgrounds and they have many different reasons for wanting to start grief groups. Some individuals experienced a death themselves when they were children and they understand what it means to have no support. Others are dealing with a more current death and want to establish something for the children. Many attendees are chaplains, therapists, school staff, hospice nurses, hospital staff, or funeral home employees. Some attendees are not trained in the mental health field at all but are caring individuals who are touched by or want to help grieving children and their families. No matter their backgrounds, they come to The Dougy Center to learn about the model and how to get one set up in their community. The following examples illustrate the variety of individuals from other countries and cultures who are drawn to The Dougy Center trainings.

Anita Paden took The Dougy Center's International Summer Institute training in 1997 and again in 1999. She became a volunteer at the Center, which inspired her to realize a longtime dream of helping grieving children in her childhood home in Central Africa. Anita was five years old when her mother, a Swedish missionary, died of pneumonia in the Congo. "I didn't have people to talk to when my mom died, so I didn't get to grieve until I was much older," recalled Anita, who has always felt a need to help others who are grieving. Anita and her husband, Bruce, have lived in Rwanda and The Democratic Republic of Congo much of their lives. They were living in the United States in the 1990s during a time when Rwanda and The Congo experienced massive killings of epic proportions. Thousands of children were orphaned during the genocide. Some witnessed the death of their entire family.

In 1999 Anita and Bruce returned to Rwanda, equipped with skills and strategies acquired from The Dougy Center's trainings. Having been missionaries in Africa since 1971, they were well aware of the challenges in starting a program for grieving children. To their surprise and delight, they immediately networked with Eugene Butera, a school administrator from Kigali, Rwanda, who had also visited The Dougy Center to learn about helping grieving children and teens. By December 1999, Anita and Eugene had launched weekly, one-hour groups for children ages six to twelve. A 2001 issue of The Dougy Center newsletter described their early successes:

ANITA PADEN

The sandbox is popular with the children in this support group in the Congo. They often play "funeral," using the two wooden crosses, two toy caskets, toy animals, and more to express how they feel.

At first, the children were naturally apprehensive about sharing their experiences. In fact, many of their parents had been at war with one another because of their ethnic affiliations. "They didn't know who they could trust, or who was their enemy and who was their friend," Anita recalled. But before long, children were sharing their stories, often in vivid detail, with crayons and pencils. Some played out their experiences in a sand box with plastic soldiers. Eventually, they talked and told one another of the horrors they had been through and how they survived. They comforted one another and experienced the powerful discovery they weren't alone. In addition, teachers began to notice the children "coming back to life." They started to make eye contact again. Their concentration improved in schoolwork. They played more.

In 2006, the Padens, along with volunteers, broke ground on the *Nouvel Espoir*, (French for "New Hope Center") located in Goma, Congo. Their work at *Nouvel Espoir* includes support groups for children and teens, as well as training and education. This support of grieving children has now spread to schools in local villages, including one school that holds fifteen grief support groups for their students.

On January 17, 1995 the Japanese port city of Kobe was struck by the Great Hanshin Earthquake, leaving more than 6,000 dead and citywide devastation. An estimated 570 children witnessed both of their parents die in the early morning quake, and several thousand more witnessed the death of one parent.

In response to the tragedy, a nonprofit program in Tokyo called *Ashinaga* initiated an outreach program to the children orphaned or impacted by a parent's death or disablement. Since 1969, *Ashinaga* has provided more than 60,000 Japanese orphans with college scholarship support, including dormitory room and board for many. (The word "orphan" in Japanese has a broader definition that includes children who have had one parent die or a parent incapacitated, as well as those who have had both parents die.)

Although no one at The Dougy Center knew at the time, ABC's "20/20" television segment on the Center had been translated and aired on Japanese television. Mr. Tamai, the director of *Ashinaga*, had seen the show. He found that The Dougy Center children interviewed on "20/20" spoke about experiences and feelings remarkably similar to the children in *Ashinaga's* program. A year later, *Ashinaga* staff began visiting The Dougy Center to learn more about setting up a program for grieving children—a radical concept in Japanese culture that broke from the ingrained tradition of stoicism in the face of tragedy.

Almost four years after the earthquake, Rainbow House opened in Kobe. It is a 22,000-square-foot, five-floor facility for a grieving children's program that includes a dormitory for college students who are also grieving due to a parent's death. The college students at *Ashinaga* volunteer about three hours a day for the program, doing chores, raising funds, cleaning, and assisting with the children who attend support groups.

Donna Schuurman attended the opening ceremony for Rainbow House. In a Dougy Center newsletter article she wrote:

> During my visit to Kobe for the opening of Rainbow House, the most moving and profound time was four hours with the bereaved college students. Their vulnerability, trust, sincerity, fears, joys, and concerns were revealed in such a trusting manner that I felt, as I often feel in The Dougy Center's groups, truly blessed to be able to share in and witness such important moments of the soul.
>
> …As they shared, it became clear that despite any cultural differences, loss is loss, pain is pain, and there is a common ground forged by grief, which transcends time, status, beliefs, ethnicity, gender, and other differentiating qualities that often separate souls.

Since then, *Ashinaga's* services have grown to another Rainbow House located in Tokyo, as well as summer camps for grieving children worldwide. As a part of its vision, *Ashinaga* states on its web site, "We at *Ashinaga* would like to be The Dougy Center of Japan." They are well on their way.

Continuing the Vision

Over the years it has been my privilege to speak at special Dougy Center events and fund-raisers, as well as speak with attendees in the opening session of the International Summer Institute. I continue to enjoy sharing the initial vision that created The Dougy Center, as well as my continuing passion for the program. More often than not I share tears and hugs with those attending the International Summer Institute, realizing we all carry the vision of a safe place for grieving children to meet and heal. Continually, I am amazed with how far the Center's outreach extends. My gratitude keeps growing for all those who work or volunteer at the Center and continue to move The Dougy Center's vision forward throughout the world.

AFTERWORD

From Ripples to Waves

Water has fascinated me since early childhood. I swam, taught swimming, life guarded, and often boated on the Iowa River during my childhood summers. As a youngster I often spent time sitting by a quiet river, lake, or pond tossing pebbles and larger stones into the water and watching the ripples radiate. As the ripples spread in ever-widening circles, I wondered, *Where do the ripples end? Do they continue even after I can no longer see the tiny waves? What effect do these ripples have on the river or pond, if any?*

Today, in the eighth decade of my life, I am once again pondering the ripple effect—this time with my journey on the winding river that led to the inception of The Dougy Center, and what it has become. Perhaps you could say that Bev Fulk and I were the ones who threw the pebble into the river that started The Dougy Center. How far our efforts would reach we did not have the slightest clue. We only knew what was in front of us—a huge river of grief with children drowning in their isolation and unrecognized sorrow.

Our vision grew and expanded, reaching further and further as others began to join us. My husband and best friend, Allan, and my mentor and friend, Elisabeth, were close by my side. They still are, in spirit. Over the years, the ripples have spread far beyond what I could ever have imagined. The hard work by the staff and volunteers at The Dougy Center continued to transform the ripples into waves, touching almost every continent. It is overwhelming to think that this program, which began in our living room with four little boys in 1982, has now spread virtually around the world. Yes, The Dougy Center was the first of its kind, and evidently it was supposed to happen. Even so, it still amazes me after all these years. And I am so grateful!

I now understand, and trust, that the ripples continue long after I can no longer see the waves. Perhaps they go on forever....

Allan and Bev Chappell

About the Author

Eric Griswold

Beverly Chappell co-founded The Dougy Center in 1982. At a time when children's grief was largely disregarded or unrecognized by many in the helping professions, Bev drew tremendous support from her mentor and friend, Elisabeth Kübler-Ross, M.D. The Center, located in Portland, Oregon, is believed to be the first center specifically for grieving children. Through the efforts of many others who share Bev's dream and carried it forward, today about 165 centers patterned after The Dougy Center span the globe.

Bev worked at the The Dougy Center for about ten years, serving as its first executive director for nearly six years. She also facilitated various children's support groups, and to this day continues to support the Center's efforts. She has taught many classes and workshops on death and grief, and has been recognized for her pioneering work in children's grief. In 2003, she received the "Distinguished Alumni Award" from Marylhurst Alumni Association for her "outstanding service to society." The Dougy Center has also honored Bev for her contributions. Bev particularly treasures one award she received from the children. A ceramic tray made at the Center reads: "For Bev—Thanks for The Dougy Center. From all the kids it helps."

Bev Chappell graduated from Iowa Methodist Hospital School of Nursing in 1951, and received her Bachelor of Arts from Marylhurst University in 1979. She was married to pediatrician Allan Chappell for forty-one years. He was a major support in the early years of The Dougy Center. She has lived in Portland since 1954, and has two children and four grandchildren.

To learn more about The Dougy Center call toll free at
866-775-5683 or visit their web site: www.dougy.org.

Index

Other Titles by NewSage Press

NewSage Press publishes nonfiction books on a variety of topics. The following books address death and grief. For a complete list of our titles, including chapter excerpts, visit our website: www.newsagepress.com

BOOKS ON HUMAN LOSS

Tea with Elisabeth: Recollections & Photographs of Dr. Elisabeth Kubler-Ross
Compiled by Fern Stewart Welch, Rose Winters & Kenneth Ross
(Available Fall 2008)

Compassion in Dying: Stories of Dignity and Choice
Barbara Coombs Lee, Ed., Foreword by Barbara K. Roberts

Death Without Denial, Grief Without Apology: A Guide for Facing Death and Loss
Barbara K. Roberts

Common Heroes: Facing a Life Threatening Illness
Eric Blau, M.D.

Life Touches Life: A Mother's Story of Stillbirth and Healing
Lorraine Ash, Foreword by Christiane Northrup, M.D.

BOOKS ON PET LOSS

Blessing the Bridge: What Animals Teach Us About Death, Dying, and Beyond
Rita Reynolds, Foreword by Gary Kowalski

Three Cats, Two Dogs, One Journey Through Multiple Pet Loss
David Congalton

NEWSAGE PRESS
PO Box 607, Troutdale, OR 97060-0607
Phone Toll Free 877-695-2211, Fax 503-695-5406
Email: info@newsagepress.com, or
www.newsagepress.com